The Meaning of
DREAMING

THE DEEPER TEACHINGS OF YOGA
ON WHY WE DREAM

The Meaning of
DREAMING

THE DEEPER TEACHINGS OF YOGA
ON WHY WE DREAM

As Explained By Paramhansa Yogananda

NAYASWAMI SAVITRI SIMPSON

 crystal clarity **publishers**

Crystal Clarity Publishers, Nevada City, CA 95959

Printed in U.S.A.
ISBN: 978-1-56589-306-1
eISBN: 978-1-56589-562-1

Cover and interior designed by David C. Jensen

Library of Congress Cataloging-in-Publication Data

Names: Simpson, Savitri, 1950- author.
Title: The meaning of dreaming : the deeper
teachings of yoga on why we dream
    as explained by Paramhansa
Yogananda / Nayaswami Savitri Simpson.
Description: Nevada City, California : Crystal
Clarity Publishers, [2016]
Identifiers: LCCN
2016006112| ISBN 9781565893061 (quality pbk. : alk.
paper)
    | ISBN 9781565895621
(ePub)
Subjects: LCSH: Self-Realization
Fellowship. | Yogananda, Paramahansa,
    1893-1952--Teachings. |
Dreams.
Classification: LCC BP605.S4 S56
2016 | DDC 135/.3--dc23
LC record available at http://lccn.loc.gov/2016006112

⊕ crystal clarity **publishers**
800.424.1055 · www.crystalclarity.com

Contents

INTRODUCTION

In the first stage of my research for this book, I was astonished by the sheer number of books and articles that have been written about dreams and dreaming—thousands, or more probably, tens of thousands! There are several websites on the topic, plus chat rooms, scientific journals, magazines, and conferences, even a whole library devoted to this subject.* At the time of my research, I found 6871 book titles on Amazon.com with the words *dream* or *dreaming* in the title.

The proliferation of available information on the subject suggests two things: first, dreams seem to be an endlessly fascinating topic for people of every culture, place, and time; and second, why should I attempt to write yet another book on the subject, when so much has already been written? In answer to this question, my research also helped me to see that, at least as well as I could determine, no one has addressed this topic in the same way that the great exponents of yoga have done. And, to my knowledge, no one has spoken or written on this subject with such fresh insights, clarity, and absolute authority as one of the greatest yoga masters of recent times, Paramhansa Yogananda.

Paramhansa Yogananda was the first yogi from India to make his permanent residence in America. Born in 1893, Yogananda

---

* A fine website for learning more about current dream research is www.asdreams.org, which is run by the International Association for the Study of Dreams.

came to the United States in 1920, where he lived until his passing in 1952. In addition to lecturing and teaching extensively in the West, he also wrote books and lessons on yoga teachings, meditation, and philosophy. In some of his earliest lessons he wrote about dreams, why we dream, and what our dreams mean. He did not write as someone presenting a theory about what dreaming is, but as a master of himself—one who had experienced every level of consciousness *consciously,* and who had achieved superconscious union with God, as well as power over life and death. In 1948 Yogananda published his masterpiece and his most important written work, *Autobiography of a Yogi,* which remains, to this day, one of the most sought-after and influential books in the annals of metaphysics.

Much of the material in this book is taken from a series of lessons Yognananda wrote in the 1920s and 1930s. Occasionally sentences, redundant in the present context, have been deleted. Sometimes words or punctuation have been changed to clarify the meaning.

In this book I also quote extensively from the books, lessons, and lectures of Swami Kriyananda (J. Donald Walters; 1926–2013), a direct disciple of Paramhansa Yogananda and my spiritual teacher for thirty-eight years. He was the founder of Ananda Sangha and its communities and centers worldwide. For nearly six decades he served Yogananda's worldwide mission through writing, lecturing, and teaching.

He is renowned also as a gifted author and composer. His published books number over a hundred, the best known of which are: *The New Path: My Life with Paramhansa Yogananda; Rays of the One Light; The Essence of Self-Realization: The Wisdom of Paramhansa Yogananda; Paramhansa Yogananda: A Biography; The Rubaiyat of Omar Khayyaam Explained; The Hindu Way of Awakening; Hope for a Better World; God is for Everyone; Conversations with Yogananda; The Essence of the Bhagavad Gita;* and *Revelations of Christ.*

What Is a Dream?

The word "dream" has several meanings. At night we fall asleep and dream. But we also use the words "dreaming" or "dreams" to describe things we are wishing to have happen, imaginations, or visualizations of desires. Another meaning suggests something insubstantial or not quite real. Paramhansa Yogananda often referred to "the dream nature of the universe," explaining that the reality of the material universe is not as real or solid as we think. Most people have had the experience, even if only for a few moments, of their life and what is going on around them having a dreamlike or insubstantial quality. People who are not grounded or are vague in their approach to life are often called "dreamy" or "dreamers."

In whatever ways we use the word, there are probably few people who have not wondered about their dreams, what they mean, or why we dream in the first place. Scientists who study sleep patterns and dream states agree that everyone dreams, even if some people say they are unable to remember their dreams. Even animals seem to dream, as evidenced by their twitching limbs, other movements, or vocalizations made while asleep. And yet this universal activity is still, in many ways, an unexplained phenomenon. This book, based on the teachings of yoga and especially those of Paramhansa Yogananda, is an attempt to demystify dreaming and what dreams mean, and to throw a new light on this ever-fascinating subject.

CHAPTER ONE

What Science Knows About Dreaming

The little centuries of human years are but days, nay, but a few hours in God's consciousness. Awaken! Arise from dreams of littleness to the realization of the vastness within you.

—Paramhansa Yogananda, *Praecepta Lessons*, Vol. 4 (1938) Praeceptum #103, 2005

What is a dream? Common definitions say that dreams are a series of images, ideas, and emotions occurring in certain stages of sleep. Dreams may take the form of a reverie, a state of abstraction, a trance, or a fantasy. Also, to dream is to hope for or imagine something, to pass time idly in reverie, to invent something, or to concoct a fantasy.

It is interesting that the root of the word "dream" is thought to be from the Germanic word "dhreugh," meaning a vision or illusion based in joy, gladness, and music.

Science and Dreams

What does the scientific community know about dreaming? Most scientists will candidly answer this question with a simple statement: "Very little!" The reason for this lack of knowledge is easy to understand. As dream researchers often explain, dreams cannot be studied objectively because they are entirely subjective.

Another way of explaining this difficulty is that there is a difference between the dream itself and the "reported dream," which can never be exactly the same. At the moment of waking from a dream, even if only seconds pass between ceasing to dream and reporting or writing the dream down, there has been a major shift of consciousness from the subconscious or REM (rapid eye movement) state of sleep to the state of conscious awareness and "awakeness." The levels of energy associated with these two states of consciousness (subconsciousness and consciousness) are different (as we will see in greater detail in a later chapter), as are the mental processes we use while experiencing them. Thus our perceptions of a dream would vary greatly, depending on our state of consciousness.

Sleep Cycles

Even though we can see the difficulty in studying dreams and dreaming on a purely scientific level, science has been able to describe clearly what the sleep-dream state is like, physiologically. This is very helpful knowledge, since most of us, on average, spend about one-third of our lives sleeping. Nearly all of us must sleep.

During normal sleep we cycle between two main types of sleep: "dream sleep" and "non-dream sleep." Both types have specific characteristics that make them easy to distinguish. Dream sleep, also referred to as REM (rapid eye movement) sleep, is sleep during which your brain is very active and you may experience dreaming. Curiously, despite the increased brain activity, your body is essentially non-moving and your muscles are completely relaxed. Your pulse rate and breathing, however, tend to increase. Also, your eyes are moving underneath closed eyelids, hence the term "rapid eye movement," abbreviated as REM sleep.

The remainder of your sleep time is composed of non-dream

or non-REM sleep. Non-REM sleep is a state of deep rest which includes the slowing of your pulse rate and respirations. Your brain activity is low. In non-REM sleep you typically pass through several stages from light sleep to deep sleep (see below for an outline of these stages)

In a normal night's sleep, every ninety minutes we experience a full sleep cycle consisting of REM sleep and all four stages of non-REM sleep. Then a new cycle starts. Typically people have four to five of these ninety-minute cycles every night. As the night progresses, you will have more REM or dream sleep in each cycle and less non-REM in each ninety-minute cycle. You will likely notice more dreaming in the hours just before awakening.

Sleep scientists can tell the difference in these cycles by watching a sleeping person's "brainwave graphs," or electroencephalograms (EEGs). These cycles are named for the "brainwaves" seen on the EEG graphs.

Awake—Beta Waves

When you are awake and alert, your brainwaves are very fast, appearing to be intense and close together—giving them an almost "dark-blurred-together" look on a brainwave chart.

Most of us are aware of what it feels like to be awake as opposed to being asleep, or even in a "falling asleep" mode. When we are fully awake, we perceive the world around us through our five senses. Sensory input is processed by the brain. While awake we are constantly sorting through this sensory input, discarding what is not essential to us in the moment, using what is pertinent to make decisions, be creative, and solve problems; this involves especially the sense of sight. Our eyes are open in order to see and perceive the world around us (as opposed to the sleep state when our eyes are closed or at least not seeing in the same way—though some people are known to sleep with their eyes open or at least partially open). We hear sounds and our brains process them. We smell and taste, particularly in relation to eating or finding nourishment for ourselves. We feel through the hands and all parts of the body, reacting to pain or simply manipulating our bodies and the world we live in through ambulatory skills and manual dexterity. This whole process of being conscious or awake takes a lot of brainpower and energy, which accounts for the speed and intensity of brain wave patterns as noted on the electroencephalogram of someone who is awake.

Most of the time while we are dreaming, we think we are awake. Indeed, many dreams are vivid to the point that upon awakening from them, we may be unsure for a few moments what is "real" and what is a dream. In a dream we think that we are seeing certain scenes, we feel ourselves touching things, hearing voices or music, even eating/tasting or smelling odors of several types. Although our brainwaves while dreaming show (see the description of the REM state below) a similarity to those of the Beta (the conscious, awake state), it is evident that we are somehow in quite a different state of consciousness. When we fully awaken from a dream, we can feel the difference—there is more clarity to a conscious state than to the subconscious state of dreaming. Most dreams seem less "real" than that which we are aware of while conscious or awake.

Drowsy But Still Awake—Alpha Waves

When you are drowsy, with your eyes closed, your brainwaves look very different. They are a little more spread apart, looking like zigzag stripes.

Closing your eyes, when you feel sleepy, cuts off one of what Yogananda described as the "sense-telephones," and allows you to withdraw your energy from the constant visual sensory input of the conscious state. This helps the brainwaves begin to slow down. We use the phrase: "my eyelids feel heavy," or "my eyes are drooping; I am falling asleep," to denote this first phase of changing our level of consciousness to subconsciousness. Using the term "falling asleep" indicates that we somehow know that we are moving from a more alert, upward-reaching state of consciousness into a lower, slower, downward-sinking level of consciousness—which, for most of us, is a needed state of rest and recovery from daily life's constant barrage of sensory input.

Remember that in this alpha wave state, you are not yet asleep. The phone could ring, or someone could call you, or switch on the light in your room, or tap you on the shoulder, and you would be able to hear, see, or feel what had happened, and probably would be able to respond as needed.

While falling asleep, we often think over the events of our day or things we have seen or heard at some other time in our lives. Our imagination wanders through different scenes in an unstructured, somewhat woozy way. Creative visualizations, or thinking pleasant, positive, affirmative thoughts during this transition from "awakeness" to being fully asleep, is said by yogis to be a very important influence on the sleep/dream state which follows.

Stage 1 Sleep—Theta Waves

In Stage 1 sleep, your brainwaves get shorter and they spread out a little more. If you were awakened in Stage 1 sleep, you would probably say you had not quite fallen asleep yet. In Stage 1 sleep your eyes may roll slowly around, under your eyelids.

Stage 2 Sleep—K-Complexes and Sleep Spindles

In Stage 2 sleep, some taller brainwaves appear once in a while. Specially shaped waves begin to manifest, called K-complexes and sleep spindles, neither of which ever appears in Stage 1. If awakened during Stage 2, you would probably agree that you had been sleeping.

"Stage 1 Sleep/Theta Waves" and "Stage 2/K-Complexes" are the next part of the falling asleep process. The difference is slight but is summed up by your perception of whether you are asleep or not yet asleep. In Stage 1 you are beginning to sleep but not deeply enough to know it should you be awakened from that state. But if you were awakened while in Stage 2, you would *know* you had been asleep, even if only for a very short time.

These two states are interesting in the light of what the great yoga masters say about levels of consciousness: that we are never fully unconscious. Even when in the deepest state of sleep, we are still conscious. Thus when we wake up from a full night's sleep or even from a short nap, we generally know something of our sleeping patterns or the quality of our sleep state—whether we slept well or restlessly, whether we were dreaming a lot or a little, the quality or content of our dreams, and so on.

Slow Wave Sleep—Delta Waves

In this stage of sleep, our brainwaves slow down and get much bigger and wider. It might be difficult to awaken us from this kind of sleep, as it is the deepest sleep state of the night. This state of sleep allows the best possible rest for an ordinary person. Almost all of the energy, which generally enlivens the senses, is withdrawn into the deepest parts of the spine and brain. There are no thoughts or dreams during this sleep state. Some mystics have called this state "the little death," for it is as close as most of us get during daily life to a complete cessation of all our faculties. Our brainwaves are slower, bigger, and wider, our hearts beat more slowly, our breathing patterns are slower and deeper, and our bodies remain stiller and unmoving for longer periods of time, than at any other time of the day or night. This state of sleep is the most refreshing we experience and ordinarily comes to us not too long after we fall asleep. It seems that we need to recharge ourselves during this state of consciousness early in our sleeping time, in order to be ready for the more active sleep states of REM/dream state that follow. (See below.)

It is interesting that yogis sometimes call this stage of sleep *turiya* or semi-superconsciousness. It mimics a true state of superconsciousness. Yogis explain that superconsciousness is a state of greater, higher awareness, an awareness of our God-nature, an awareness of our connection with the great Cosmic Source of all that is. This state is achieved and maintained primarily through meditation, but it is also experienced by people at various times in their lives, though it may not be identified by the word "superconsciousness."

The reason for the "semi-" part of the term "semi-superconsciousness" is that, even though it is by its nature a very spiritual state of consciousness, it is still a *passive* state of consciousness, into which we fall (must fall!) each night. The yoga sciences teach us how to evoke a state of true superconsciousness which is even more "recharging" in its nature than semi-superconsciousness, for it is not in any way passive. That state is actively achieved and much more clearly perceived. You don't *fall* into superconsciousness. Instead you consciously *rise* into that state, primarily through deep meditation and the grace of God. Once experienced, superconsciousness becomes infinitely more desirable than semi-superconsciousness. This is because it is a much higher state of consciousness wherein, as Yogananda wrote, the "knower, knowing, and known are one." We will discuss the various states of consciousness, including superconsciousness, in a later chapter.

Many sleep studies have shown that this "delta wave," deepest state of sleep seems essential to mental and physical health. The yogic teachings would agree, saying that semi-superconsciousness is the time during which we tap into our origins, our essential state of being, and our divine nature. We *must* do this often (preferably nightly) in order to recharge our spiritual batteries, or we cannot go on with our lives. We all know something of the dangers and suffering caused by sleep deprivation. Not being able to experience semi-superconsciousness causes all manner of mental/

physical disturbances. It seems clear that the reason for this is that, although we certainly have mental and physical aspects to our beings, our truest and deepest nature is essentially spiritual. From this "spiritual being" or Higher Self, which yoga speaks of so often, spring all the other states of consciousness. It is through contacting this Higher Self, through deep sleep or in prayer and meditation, that we find true rest and freedom.

Thus we can see that the delta-wave state is important beyond what most scientists understand about sleep states. It is indeed "sweet" and refreshing. It allows us to relax completely and let go of the world of sensory input and the activities or responsibilities of daily life. Even more importantly it offers us, even for a short time, a way to tap into the essence of who and what we really are.

REM Sleep

In Rapid Eye Movement (REM) sleep, your brainwaves are small and fast again, as in Stage 1. But now a striking new physiological phenomenon occurs: while the rest of your body remains relatively still, your eyes begin to make sharp movements under your eyelids. This is a good thing, because most dreaming occurs during REM sleep, and it would be inconvenient, to say the least, if one's body started acting out all of one's dreams in physical movements.

It has been shown in many sleep studies that all dreaming is accompanied by eye movements. Because of this, dream-researchers have been able to determine that dreaming seems a very necessary and normal activity for most people, whether or not they remember their dreams. This necessity was demonstrated in laboratory tests during which sleepers were awakened every time "Rapid Eye Movement" began to take place. After a few days of allowing them to sleep, but not to go into the dream (REM) state, the subjects began to show signs of mental illness and breakdown. These experiments seem to indicate that both dreaming and the deeper delta-wave sleep state are necessary to maintain psychological and physical health.

These are the physical indications that dreams are taking place during the state of consciousness we call sleep. These dreams are very different from what we call daydreaming. Daydreaming is a more conscious or active way of using, during the waking state, our creative imagination. In a daydreaming state, our eyes may be open or closed, but we are most definitely awake.

Brain Mapping

Scientists today are further decoding the biology of the brain and how it looks as it manufactures dreams. This is being done through medical devices such as PET scans, wherein colorful "maps" of the brain and its changing energetic outputs may be photographed, charted, and analyzed. The part of the brain that most actively "lights up" during nightly dreams is the limbic or primitive ("low road" emotion) brain. Paramhansa Yogananda taught that the medulla oblongata (located at the base of the brain) is the "seat of the ego, or the little self"; this area of the brain is suffused with subconscious activities such as fight-or-flight instincts and positive/negative emotions. These subconscious brain activities direct the majority of our nightly dream patterns.

The PET scan studies also show that the frontal lobes of the brain disengage when one is dreaming. The yoga teachings have always referred to the front of the brow as a "chakra" or energy center which, when concentrated upon and awakened through meditation practices, offers superconscious, rather than subconscious awareness. This part of the brain is the "seat of the Higher Self" or "a place of enlightenment." Though dreams or visions may occasionally come from the superconscious Self, most dreams have their origin in the little self—that is, the egoic or more subconscious part of the brain. With increased depth of meditation, even our dreams can change their place of origin and offer us superconscious bliss rather than subconscious ramblings.

Interesting though this scientifically based information about sleeping and dreaming may be, it leaves aside the primary question of why, when asleep, we dream. The great yoga masters, and more particularly Paramhansa Yogananda, have a definite answer to this question, and it is both similar to and goes far beyond the answers offered by scientists or psychiatrists. But before we present their teachings on this subject, let's look at a few other interesting theories.

Theories About Why We Dream

The following speculations about why we dream have been compiled from the writings of many scientists, psychologists, and specialists in sleep/dream studies, and metaphysicians from various religious and cultural backgrounds. Many of these theories have a certain amount of merit to them, in relation to the yogic teachings—some more than others.

In the yoga tradition, there is a process of discernment or discrimination called *neti, neti,* meaning "not this, not that." Through the *neti, neti* process you examine each of the possible solutions to a question, tossing out the ones which don't prove true or worthwhile, until you come to the essence or the answer to your question. Let us now apply *neti, neti* to these theories, until we arrive at what this book presents as the final and truest reason for why we dream.

Dreams help to diffuse or soothe our moods. During the day we are swayed by our emotions, attachments, and likes and dislikes, all of which cause positive and negative moods. This process is like being constantly tossed about on a restless ocean. We may grow somewhat used to being tossed about by these waves, but eventually we grow tired of it and seek calm waters so that we might rest and let go of moods and what causes them. Dreams certainly may include moods, but most of the time those moods do not involve or drain us as dramatically as the ones that may haunt us in daily life.

Dreams help us with memory consolidation. When we dream we are ordinarily in a subconscious state. Our subconscious has many functions, as we will see later in this book, and one of the most important of these functions is to store memories of every event or thought that occurs in every moment of our lives. We can see how this recording process could create massive amounts of information, and that this information would need to be stored somewhere in our brains. So it is natural to theorize that a sorting, consolidating, and storing-away-for-future-use process might be a very handy activity to go through on a nightly basis. Otherwise we would be overwhelmed with memories and unable to function in the present moment. The dreaming process may help us determine which memories to keep closer to the surface of our consciousness and which to put into "deep storage" in our subconscious.

Dreams help us to fix new memories in the brain and connect them with old memories. As memories are being generated constantly during our waking hours, it would be reasonable to assume that, because there are so many of them, a process of relating new memories to the old ones already stored in the brain and nervous system would be helpful and time-saving. This might take place in part during the dream state. For example, if, during your day, you saw a dog which looked dangerous, then during your dream state you dreamed of a dog which attacked you when you were a child, your subconscious would bond these memories together with the conclusion that, in future, when you see a dog acting in a certain way, it implies danger and appropriate action must be taken to ensure your safety.

Neural growth and important brain-connections may take place while dreaming. Science knows a lot more now about the way our brains work, and is learning more with each passing year. One most important piece of information, which has been proved in recent brain studies, is that the brain is in a constant state of growth and change. Certain synapses or brain-cell connections are enhanced more powerfully during certain mental or physical activities. So it is possible, though unproven yet, that dreaming is one of the activities which makes neural growth happen, even while we rest and sleep.

Personality or character development takes place while we dream; dreams can spur us to new and vigorous adventures or personal growth, help form or strengthen our personalities, or offer us self-confidence and self-understanding. Almost everyone has experienced dreams in which we find ourselves doing something we would not want or be able to do; or doing something we might have wanted to do, but have not had the courage or abilities to do—visiting places we have never been, meeting people we have never met, or having conversations with people that we wanted to have (but have not yet had the courage to speak our minds), or facing disasters or challenges which might be coming to us. Dreams may provide us with dress rehearsals for life situations yet to happen, and thus strengthen our emotional ability to meet them, if and when they come to us. In other words, we act out in our dreams that which we have not yet been able to accomplish during the waking state. This process could help us to develop strength of character or personality, or the courage to make needed changes in our lives.

Here is an interesting dream, related by Swami Kriyananda, which might more clearly exemplify these theories. This story is taken from chapter 9 of his autobiography, *The New Path*, and is called "The Torture Chamber Dream."

"[In my dream] I was living with many other people in a torture chamber. For generations our families had lived here, knowing no world but this one; the possibility of any other existence simply never occurred to us. One awoke, one was tortured, and, at night, one found brief respite in sleep. What else could there be to life? We didn't particularly mind our lot. Rather, we imagined ourselves reasonably well-off. Oh, to be sure, there were bad days, but then there were also good ones—days together, sometimes, when we were less tortured than usual.

"The time came, however, when a handful of us began to think the unthinkable. Might there, we asked ourselves, just possibly be *another*, a better way of life? Moments snatched when our torturers were out of earshot, and we could share our doubts with a few friends, served to kindle our speculations. At last we determined that there simply *had* to be an alternative to being tortured. A small group of us decided to rebel.

"We laid our plans carefully. One day, rising together from our tasks, we slipped up behind the torturers, slew them, and escaped. Sneaking cautiously out of the great room, fearing lest armies of torturers be lying in wait for us outside, we encountered no one. The torture chamber itself, it turned out, occupied only the top floor of a large, otherwise empty building. We walked unchallenged down flights of stairs, emerging from the ground floor onto a vast, empty plain. Confined as we'd been our whole lives in the torture chamber, the horizon seemed incredibly distant. Joyfully we inhaled the fresh air. Gazing about us, we all but shouted the previously never-imagined word: 'Freedom!'

"Before departing the building forever, we glanced up at the top floor, scene of the only life we'd ever known. There, to our astonishment, we saw the very torturers we thought we'd slain. They were going matter-of-factly about their business as though nothing had happened! Amazed, we looked to one another for an explanation.

"Suddenly the answer dawned on me. 'Don't you see?' I exclaimed. 'It's ourselves we have conquered, not the torturers!'

"With that realization, I awoke.

"I felt that this dream held an important message for me. The torture chamber, located as it was on the top floor of the building, symbolized the human mind. The torturers represented our mental shortcomings. The emptiness of the rest of the building meant that once one has overcome his mental torturers, there are no more enemies left to conquer. All human suffering, in other words, originates in the mind. We cannot slay universal delusion; all we can do is slay our own mental torturers. They will always remain on the scene, inflicting on others their painful lessons.

"My dream, I felt, held a divine message for me. Its implication was that the time had come for me to seek a higher way of life."

Dreams help to diffuse harmful emotions such as worries, hopes, fears, or even terror. Or they may help to overcome our frustrations, or to release the tensions and stress of the day. Perhaps we use our nightly dreams as ways to unravel the "emotional knots" we have tied in our psyches during the day. Dreams have been called our "built-in therapist." It is fairly clear that when we are feeling stressed, worried, or afraid, our dreams often reflect the same worries, fears, or stressful situations. As to whether these types of dreams can actually diffuse these emotions is another question. Perhaps they do the opposite and tend to enhance our worried and restless state of mind, when they could be better dealt with and released (or even transmuted) in other ways, such as going into a superconscious state in meditation.

My husband often tells me of what he calls his "unfinished business" dreams. For example, if his work that day involved putting in a complicated plumbing system, in his dreams that night he continues to do the same, and is often equally or even more frustrated by the "dream plumbing installation process." In the morning he relates that he definitely does not feel rested—in fact, he feels that it would have been much more productive to have tried to release these problems through meditation and prayer so that he might dream then of "higher" things than plumbing problems.

The teachings of yoga suggest that before going to bed, it would be best to clear your mind and heart through meditation techniques. Offer everything you have done or felt during the preceding day—all emotions, likes and dislikes, worries, and fears—back into God's hands.

We dream to keep our minds active at night and therefore, in the habit of being more alert at all times. The reasoning behind this theory has to do with our cavemen ancestors and the way we evolved upward from the animal state. Being alert, at least to a certain degree, even while sleeping, was a necessary survival skill for the human species. Falling nightly into eight continuous hours of the deepest sort of sleep state (delta waves) would not lend itself to survival for a caveman. It would make sense that dreaming, during a lighter state of sleep, would help keep the mind "at the ready" in case of threatened danger during darker, more dangerous hours of the night.

It has been said by the great yoga masters that the mind is similar to a muscle. When it is not used well, it tends to "atrophy," losing some of its ability to be sharp and clear in its thinking. Memories are not as easily retrieved. Recent research into the causes and cures of senility conditions such as Alzheimer's disease suggest that one preventative measure for those at risk would be to keep the mind active with reading, crossword puzzles, stimulating conversations, and other such activities. Likewise, an active dream-life may keep the "mind muscle" in good shape.

We dream for fun and entertainment. Many dreams, perhaps most of them, may be classified as entertaining or enjoyable. The feeling of waking from such a dream is pleasant and often amusing, making us smile at the absurdities of life. The "heaviness" of life's daily responsibilities may be lightened by seeking out entertainment through humorous reading materials, television, movies, circuses, plays—those activities which make us laugh and forget our troubles for a while. So too, dreams may help us relax and lighten up. Many times, upon first awakening in the mornings, I have related an entertaining dream to my husband. We laugh together over the absurdities of my dream, and that laughter feels very healing and refreshing. Yogananda clearly states, as we'll discuss in a later chapter, that all of life is given to instruct and entertain us. Our dream-life may similarly instruct us, but more often it is simply meant to entertain us. A lifetime full of nightly sleep, without any dreams to spice it up, might be extremely dull. The human mind seems to need constant stimulation, if not entertainment.

Dreams are caused by overeating, late or heavy meals, or highly spiced foods. Most of us have experienced wild dreams or nightmares after eating particularly rich, heavy, or sweet foods soon before bed. Yogic teachings are very specific about keeping our digestive systems healthy through special diet, fasting, and eating at specific times. The Western tradition of eating three full meals a day is often not the healthiest course of action, especially when we eat the heaviest meal in the evening. To go to sleep on a full stomach is to create a conflict of interests in the way we use our energy. When we eat, large amounts of our life force are needed in our digestive tracts to take care of the complex processes of changing food into energy. We should wait several hours after a full meal before going to sleep. Yogananda's suggestions for proper eating patterns are stated in this way: "Eat like a prince for breakfast, a king for lunch, and a pauper for dinner (supper)."

Dreams may occur in order to reinforce our creativity and the way we associate ideas in our minds; one thing links to another and another and another. Dreams often have a "wandering" quality to them, wherein we may be in the middle of a dream, and then one element of the dream leads us into an entirely different dream sequence, and then another, and another. This process may reflect or even strengthen our mind's creative abilities. The dream ability to constantly connect things together in new sequences may keep our minds fresh and able to see things in new and different ways.

Many religious and spiritual traditions teach that dreams are highly symbolic and meaningful; that they can offer predictions and guidance for the future; that they can represent divine intervention (God speaking to us through our dreams); and that dreams can help us understand our relationship with life or with God. There are many examples in religious history of such dreams. In chapter 3 of this book, "Dreaming Through the Ages," we will offer several interesting examples of this aspect of dreaming.

Dreams may serve as a way for our subconscious mind to come up with solutions to problems. Most people have had an experience of overcoming, solving, or at least lessening a major life challenge by "sleeping on it." Sometimes, while sleeping, a dream will give us an important key to understanding what is needed to deal successfully with a problem.

Elias Howe, the inventor of the sewing machine, reported an amazing example of a dream-created solution. Mr. Howe said that he received the breakthrough concept for the sewing machine in a dream. He fell asleep after puzzling for a long time over how to solve the problem of placing a needle into a machine so that it would automatically push the thread through the cloth. It seemed impossible to accomplish this function, because of where the "thread-hole" of a regular needle was located.

In his dream, cannibals had captured him. As they were preparing to cook and eat him, they were dancing around the fire waving their spears. Howe noticed that near the tip of each spear was a small hole. The image of the hole's unusual location and the up-and-down motion of the spears remained with him when he woke.

Thus the innovative idea of passing the thread through a needle close to its tip, rather than through the other end, made possible the mechanical sewing machine.

And finally, *some who have thoroughly studied this subject have speculated that we dream for no good reason at all.* This theory would seem the most difficult to accept, from a commonsense point of view. If there were no reason to dream, we probably wouldn't! Living beings do not often waste time and energy in activities that have no function, even if that function is just to have fun, or to do something creative and different. It would be hard to refute the fact that human beings somehow need to dream, and that the process of dreaming reveals an important creative aspect of the way our minds and lives function. If we accept that we were molded by a Divine Creator and also formed "in God's image," then obviously our Creator has given us the ability to dream for some specific purpose.

CHAPTER TWO

More Information About Dreaming

I am the prince of perpetual peace playing in a drama of sad and happy dreams on the stage of experience.

—from *Metaphysical Meditations* (1932 Edition) by Paramhansa Yogananda

Everybody Dreams!

One interesting question we may ask about dreaming is: "Does everyone dream?" Science agrees with the yogis that the answer is: "Yes!" Laboratory studies have shown that everyone experiences the REM state of sleep, when dreams primarily occur. Under laboratory-controlled conditions, all those who claimed to be "non-dreamers," when awakened from REM-sleep, agreed that they were dreaming.

"What If I Don't Remember My Dreams?"

If it is true that everyone dreams, why do some people have trouble remembering their dreams? One clue is that "non-rememberers" take much longer to awaken from sleep than those who have less trouble remembering. Perhaps this added time at the end of their sleep cycles erases their connection to what they might have been dreaming. Or perhaps it has something to do with visualization, imagination, or memory capabilities, or even the desire (or lack of it) to remember one's dreams. Dreams are perceived as enjoyable and entertaining by some and not so by others. Some people have no difficulty in remembering several dreams nightly, whereas others recall dreams only occasionally or not at all.

Then, too, a "non-rememberer" may be the type of person who deals with his problems and challenges by denying or forgetting them—avoiding the awareness of uncomfortable emotions and desires, and practiced in forgetting them—such a person may extend this practice to dreams also, becoming an "efficient forgetter."

"Are we all equally imaginative in our sleep, or do people who are already creative in their waking hours retain that edge at night? Much as it would be nice to think that sleep is a great democratizer, the fact is, creative types seem to have an advantage in the dream-remembering process. Psychologist David Watson of Notre Dame tracked 200 subjects over three months and found that those who scored high on creativity scales when they were awake tended to remember their dreams more. 'One reason is that they simply have more vivid and interesting dreams,' he says. 'That's linked to having creative daytime behavior patterns, which shade over into the night. This is a case of the rich getting richer.'"*

In any case, what happens during sleep—including dreams, thoughts that occur throughout the night, or memories of brief awakenings—is often forgotten by morning. There is something about the phenomenon of sleep which makes it difficult to remember what has occurred. Most dreams are soon forgotten unless they are quite emotionally or spiritually impactful—or are written down. Sometimes a dream is suddenly remembered later in the day or in the future, suggesting that the memory of a dream is not totally lost, just a labor to retrieve.

* From an article titled "How Sleep Can Spark Creativity," *Time* magazine, April 23, 2012:

Improving One's Ability to Remember Dreams

In many dream studies, it has been shown that it is possible to improve your dream-memory process. Before you fall asleep, remind yourself that you want to remember your dreams. Keep a paper and pen or a voice-recorder by your bedside. As you awaken, try to move as little as possible, and try not to start thinking about other things. Write down what you can remember of your dream images—and do it swiftly as they can fade quickly if not recorded. Any distraction probably will cause the memory of your dream to be lost. If you can't remember a full dream, just put down what you can recall, even if you have only a vague impression of it.

Why do memories of most of our dreams fade away so quickly? It is probably because we simply don't want or need to remember most of them on the conscious level—they are just not that important to us. The conscious brains of most human beings become "overloaded" with too much sensory input. Thus our memories, including those of our dreams, are stored in the subconscious—our psychological storage vault.

Dreaming in Color

Most dreams are in color, although people may not be aware of it, either because they have difficulty remembering their dreams or because color is such a natural part of visual experience that they don't make note of it in a dream. Recent studies show that about eighty percent of people dream in color, though only a quarter of that number recall, upon awakening, the exact shades of color.

People who are more visually oriented (artists for example), or those who are very aware of color while awake, probably notice color more often in their dreams. If you feel you do not dream "in color" but would like to, try this experiment. Before you fall asleep, affirm: "I will remember at least one color from the dreams I dream tonight." Then, immediately upon awakening from a dream, carefully remember one item in the dream that should have a color you would easily remember or notice, such as the sky, a flower, or a car. Then jot it down before you forget it. Doing this frequently should help you become more aware of the colors in your dreams.

In the February 2006 edition of *Reader's Digest* is a report on an Arizona-based researcher named Robert Hoss, who claims to accurately predict people's emotional states by analyzing the color patterns in their dreams.

Dreaming the Same Dreams Over and Over

If we have a frequently recurring dream, it would make sense that there might be a special message for us in that dream. It can be helpful to look for parallels between the dream and the thoughts, feelings, behavior, and motives of the dreamer. Understanding the meaning of a recurrent dream may help the dreamer resolve an issue that he or she has been struggling with for years. In chapter 10 we'll offer suggestions and techniques for understanding the meaning of a specific dream or dream images and symbols. These techniques can be especially important in finding the meaning or message of a recurrent dream.

Nightmares

Nightmares are very common among children and fairly common among adults. For adults, nightmares are thought to be caused by extreme stress, unresolved fears, indigestion, traumatic experiences, emotional difficulties, drugs or medication, or illness. However, some people have frequent nightmares that seem unrelated to any of these conditions or to their waking lives in any way. In these cases, one might speculate that their nightmares were related to "memories" from a past lifetime.

The great yoga masters tell us that our memories from past lives, though perhaps buried very deep in our sub- or superconscious beings, are with us always. This theory would also account for children more frequently experiencing nightmares than adults.

Unresolved fears or difficulties from their past lives would be "closer" to them in time. Their sensitive natures might not have been able to "screen out" past life traumas. Recent studies suggest that nightmares tend to occur in the dreams of adults or children who are more open, sensitive, trusting, and emotional than average. Prayer, meditation, strengthening and protective affirmations, and other spiritually based techniques may be helpful in dealing with nightmares.

One common "nightmare fallacy" is that if you die in your dream, or if you hit bottom in a falling dream, you will in fact die in your sleep. These ideas are not true. Many people have dreamed that they died or hit bottom in a fall, and they have lived to tell the tale! You can explore the meaning of such images just as you would explore any others that might occur in your dreams.

Dreams Which Accurately Predict the Future

There are many examples of dreams that predict future events. Some may have been due to coincidence, faulty memory, or an unconscious tying together of known information. A few laboratory studies have been conducted on predictive dreams, as well as on clairvoyant and telepathic dreams, but the results were varied, as these kinds of dreams are difficult to study in a laboratory setting.

An Example of a Predictive Dream—Abraham Lincoln

President Abraham Lincoln reported this dream to his wife, Mary, shortly before his assassination. "I retired very late. I had been up waiting for important dispatches from the front. I could not have been long in bed when I fell into a slumber, for I was weary. I soon began to dream. There seemed to be a death-like stillness about me. Then I heard subdued sobs, as if a number of people were weeping. I thought I left my bed and wandered downstairs. There the same pitiful sobbing broke the silence, but the mourners were invisible. I went from room to room; no living person was in sight, but the same mournful sounds of distress met me as I passed along. It was light in all the rooms; every object was familiar to me; but where were all the people who were grieving as if their hearts would break?

"I was puzzled and alarmed. What could be the meaning of all this? Determined to find the cause of a state of things so mysterious and so shocking, I kept on until I arrived at the East Room, which I entered. There I met with a sickening surprise. Before me was a catafalque, on which rested a corpse wrapped in funeral vestments. Around it were stationed soldiers who were acting as guards; and there was a throng of people, some gazing mournfully upon the corpse, whose face was covered, others weeping pitifully.

"'Who is dead in the White House?' I demanded of one of the soldiers.

"'The President' was his answer; 'he was killed by an assassin!' Then came a loud burst of grief from the crowd, which awoke me from my dream.'"

Controlling Our Dreams

It is believed that you can influence, if not control, your dreams by giving yourself pre-sleep suggestions. Another method of influencing dreams is called "lucid dreaming," in which you train yourself to become aware that you are dreaming, while still asleep and in the dream. Sometimes people experience lucid dreaming spontaneously. Some believe that it is possible to learn how to increase lucid dreaming, and thereby increase one's capacity to affect the course of the dream events as they unfold. Some people seem better able to control their dreams than others—it is almost as though they possess an inborn talent for it.

Complete control of one's dreams seems to be an extremely rare talent, though many yoga masters speak of this ability as not only possible, but as a skill that actually can be developed through certain yogic practices.

* Ward Hill Lamon, *Recollections of Abraham Lincoln* 1847–1865, 1911

Recent scientific experiments show that strong, pre-sleep suggestions do not *consistently* produce a specific dream, though occasionally the suggested images may appear in a dream.

A few dream workers advise against trying to control our dreams. Instead, they encourage us simply to enjoy them, learn from them as we can, and eventually move toward understanding why we dream.

We will discuss more about taking charge of our "dream-dramas" in chapter 8 of this book.

CHAPTER THREE

Dreaming Through the Ages

Beholding the elusive sound pictures, I am sure this daily-changing drama of turbulent and dancing lives is nothing but a vast dream-vitaphone presentation. World tragedies, comedies, paradoxes of life, dreams of birth and death, news of changing facts, are nothing but talking pictures, to keep all our senses and thoughts deluded and entertained. Teach me to look upon the movie-dream of my own life with a thrilling, interested attitude, so that, at the end of each picture, I may exclaim: "Ah, that was a good picture, full of thrills and life. I am pleased to have seen it, for I have learned much from it."

—from a prayer by Paramhansa Yogananda in *Inner Culture* magazine, July 1942

The History of Dream Interpretation

In the histories of most known cultures, from ancient to present times, there occur either written or oral indications of the importance of dreams and dreaming, often particularly for the leaders or "wise ones" who try to guide or keep the culture steady and intact. In more primitive cultures, the "dreamers" are considered essential to the safety, health, and welfare of the group.

One could safely say that until the late 1800s, with perhaps a few exceptions, dream interpretation was primarily an aspect of religion or a part of the metaphysical, mystical, or healing domain of a culture. Only in fairly recent times has the subject become a part of scientific studies of how the mind works, most especially through psychology and psychoanalysis.

The most fertile years in the career of Sigmund Freud were from 1895 to 1900. It was during those years that he did some of his most important research on the subconscious mind, a vast labor that culminated in the publication in 1900 of his major work, *The Interpretation of Dreams*, which was a turning point for modern concepts about dreams and what they might mean to us on a psychological level. He believed that the analysis of dreams was a very useful and powerful tool in uncovering subconscious thoughts and desires, and that the purpose of dreams is "to allow us to satisfy in fantasies the instinctual urges that society judges unacceptable."

Carl Jung's works also, though more metaphysically than scientifically based, have had a strong influence on how we think about the ever-fascinating subject of dreams and what they mean.

The Judeo-Christian Bible is filled with many reported dreams—dreams that prophesy, guide, predict, or protect people from harm.

Old Testament Dreams—Joseph, the Great Dream Interpreter

In the Old Testament, Joseph was a man whose dreams and dream interpretations shaped his life and the lives of his kinsmen. One of twelve brothers, he was his father Jacob's favorite son. Naturally this did not endear him to his elder brothers (he was next to the youngest). While still a teenage shepherd, he dreamed about eleven bundles of wheat, which "made obeisance" to Joseph's one bundle of wheat. Another dream was about the sun, moon, and stars bowing down to his star. The meaning of these dreams was fairly obvious and extremely upsetting to Joseph's brothers. Taking action, they conspired to rid themselves of young Joseph by selling him into slavery in Egypt.

Joseph's dreams came true years later, when he was miraculously released from slavery and prison and placed in a position of great power, second in command to the Egyptian Pharaoh—all of which resulted from his correct interpretations of the dreams of some of his companions and finally of Pharaoh himself. Joseph is quoted as saying, regarding his ability to interpret dreams correctly: "Surely, all my dream interpretations come from God." (Genesis 40:8)

Joseph's dream interpretations had a tremendous impact not only on Egypt, but also on the future of dream interpretations in Western civilization.

Daniel in the Kingdom of Babylon

Later in the Old Testament we read of the amazing dream interpretations of Daniel, a Jew held in captivity in Babylon during the reign of Nebuchadnezzar. Daniel rose to high estate in the final years of Nebuchadnezzar's life and retained this position during the rule of the king's successors. We are told that Nebuchadnezzar "dreamed dreams wherewith his spirit was troubled and his sleep brake from him." (Daniel 2:1 KJV) Not one of the mighty king's magicians, astrologers, sorcerers, or wise men could interpret the dream; by failing to do so, they were executed. Daniel asked for the prayers of his friends and fellow captives, after which God revealed to him the secrets of Nebuchadnezzar's dreams, and he was able to tell them to the king.

The dream was of a great and mighty statue whose head was of gold, torso and arms of silver, belly and thighs of brass, lower legs of iron, and feet of clay. The statue was smitten in the feet by a stone and the whole image collapsed (thus we recognize the origin of the idiom "feet of clay," meaning having an unstable foundation, vulnerability, failing, or weakness). Daniel correctly interpreted that the dream represented future kingdoms, which, though strong and mighty, would crumble in time because of these "feet of clay." Nebuchadnezzar was so impressed by what Daniel's God had revealed to him about this dream—Daniel didn't neglect to give all the credit to the God of Israel—that Daniel was made a lesser ruler in the kingdom. Daniel, with God's help, continued to correctly interpret many, many prophetic dreams (which always came true) for several later kings of Babylon.

King Solomon's Wonderful Dream

Another Old Testament dreamer was King Solomon. In one important dream, God appeared to him and said, "Ask what I shall give thee." (I Kings 3:5 KJV) Even more amazing was Solomon's answer. God had offered him anything he might have wished for: riches, kingdoms, good health, long life, or the death of his enemies. But Solomon asked instead for wisdom, discrimination, and an understanding heart, the better to rule his people righteously. God then said that because Solomon had asked for none of the things most people would certainly have asked for under those circumstances, all those things would be given to him, in addition to wisdom and an understanding heart. "And I have also given thee that which thou hast not asked, both riches, and honor: so that there shall not be any among the kings like unto thee all thy days." (I Kings 3:13 KJV) And since that ancient time the name King Solomon has become a symbol for one who is very rich, but also very wise.

New Testament Dreams—Concerning the Birth of Jesus

In the New Testament, many events around the birth of Jesus Christ involved dreams or visions. Zachariah, Jesus' uncle and the father of John the Baptist, was unable to speak for many months after his dream of an angel who told him of the coming birth of his son to his wife, Elizabeth—a miracle in itself, given that she was beyond her childbearing years.

Mary told her fiancé, Joseph, that she was with child. Because he knew he was not the father of the child, he wanted to hide her away. "But while he thought on these things, behold, the angel of the Lord appeared unto him in a dream, saying Joseph, thou son of David, fear not to take unto thee Mary thy wife; for that which is conceived in her is of the Holy Ghost. Then Joseph being raised from his sleep did as the angel of the Lord had bidden him, and took unto him his wife." (Matthew 2:20 KJV)

Sometime after Jesus was born to Mary and Joseph in the stable in Bethlehem, the wise men from the East came searching for him. Knowing that a special, royal baby had been born, they inquired this from Herod, the king in Jerusalem at that time. Herod knew nothing of this baby, and was very angry to hear such news. The wise men found the Holy Family without Herod's help. "And being warned of God in a dream that they should not return to Herod, [the wise men] departed into their own country another way." (Matthew 2:12 KJV)

Herod went on a rampage to find and eliminate this royal child, whom he thought might someday become a rival for his throne, by slaughtering every child in Bethlehem under the age of two. But again a nighttime warning came at just the right moment. "The angel of the Lord appeared to Joseph in a dream, saying, 'Arise, and take the young child and his mother, and flee into Egypt and be thou there until I bring thee word; for Herod will seek the young child and destroy him.'" (Matthew 2:13)

Joseph immediately took his family and departed for Egypt, where they remained until it was safe to return to their home in Nazareth.

A Divine Vision* of Paramhansa Yogananda

Paramhansa Yogananda was a man of many dreams and visions. Here is one of many such visions as described in his *Autobiography of a Yogi* (1946 edition).

Yogananda relates: "In 1915, shortly after I had entered the Swami Order, I witnessed a vision of violent contrasts. In it the relativity of human consciousness was vividly established; I clearly perceived the unity of the Eternal Light behind the painful dualities of *maya*. The vision descended on me as I sat one morning in my little attic room in Father's Gurpar Road home [in Calcutta]. For months World War I had been raging in Europe; I reflected sadly on the vast toll of death.

"As I closed my eyes in meditation, my consciousness was suddenly transferred to the body of a captain in command of a battleship. The thunder of guns split the air as shots were exchanged between shore batteries and the ship's cannons. A huge shell hit the powder magazine and tore my ship asunder. I jumped into the water, together with the few sailors who had survived the explosion.

"Heart pounding, I reached the shore safely. But alas! A stray bullet ended its furious flight in my chest. I fell groaning to the ground. My whole body was paralyzed, yet I was aware of possessing it as one is conscious of a leg gone to sleep.

"'At last the mysterious footstep of Death has caught up with me,' I thought. With a final sigh, I was about to sink into unconsciousness when lo! I found myself seated in the lotus posture in my Gurpar Road room.

"Hysterical tears poured forth as I joyfully stroked and pinched my regained possession-a body free from any bullet hole in the breast. I rocked to and fro, inhaling and exhaling to assure myself that I was alive. Amidst these self-congratulations, again I found

---

*The difference between regular nightly dreams and divine visions will be explored later in this book.

my consciousness transferred to the captain's dead body by the gory shore. Utter confusion of mind came upon me.

"'Lord,' I prayed, 'am I dead or alive?'

"A dazzling play of light filled the whole horizon. A soft rumbling vibration formed itself into words: 'What has life or death to do with Light? In the image of My Light I have made you. The relativities of life and death belong to the cosmic dream. Behold your dreamless being! Awake, my child, awake!' . . .

"[Decades later, in Encinitas, California] I sat on my bed in the lotus posture. My room was dimly lit by two shaded lamps. Lifting my gaze, I noticed that the ceiling was dotted with small mustard-colored lights, scintillating and quivering with a radium-like luster. Myriads of penciled rays, like sheets of rain, gathered into a transparent shaft and poured silently upon me.

"At once my physical body lost its grossness and became metamorphosed into astral texture. I felt a floating sensation as, barely touching the bed, the weightless body shifted slightly and alternately to left and right. I looked around the room; the furniture and walls were as usual, but the little mass of light had so multiplied that the ceiling was invisible. I was wonder-struck.

"'This is the cosmic motion picture mechanism.' A voice spoke as though from within the light. 'Shedding its beam on the white screen of your bed sheets, it is producing the picture of your body. Behold, your form is nothing but light!'

"I gazed at my arms and moved them back and forth, yet could not feel their weight. An ecstatic joy overwhelmed me. This cosmic stem of light, blossoming as my body, seemed a divine replica of the light beams streaming out of the projection booth in a cinema house and manifesting as pictures on the screen.

"For a long time I experienced this motion picture of my body in the dimly lighted theater of my own bedroom. Despite the many visions I have had, none was ever more singular. As my illusion of a solid body was completely dissipated, and my realization deepened that the essence of all objects is light, I looked up to the throbbing stream of lifetrons and spoke entreatingly.

"'Divine Light, please withdraw this, my humble bodily picture, into Thyself, even as Elijah was drawn up to heaven by a flame.'

"This prayer was evidently startling; the beam disappeared. My body resumed its normal weight and sank on the bed; the swarm of dazzling ceiling lights flickered and vanished. My time to leave this earth had apparently not arrived."

Dreams of Swami Kriyananda

"The Disincarnate Entity Dream"*

"One night [shortly after first coming to live in Yogananda's ashram], I dreamed that I was at a party. The thought suddenly came to me with striking certainty: 'It's time to go meet a disembodied spirit.' I left my friends and passed through an empty, well-lit room toward an open door on the far side. I can still see clearly in my mind's eye the bare floorboards and walls, the shining bulb dangling from the ceiling. The next room was dark; here, I knew, I was to meet the disincarnate entity. Momentarily apprehensive, I reached out to switch on the light. Then I rebuked myself, thinking, 'Don't be a coward,' and pulled back. 'How will you learn what this is all about,' I asked myself, 'if you don't dare face it?' And so, leaving the room dark, I stood in the center of it and called out, 'Come!'

"Here comes the 'gothic' part of my story. The following day Jean Haupt told me that he had been awakened at about the same time of night by a loud, fierce pounding on his door.

"'Wh-what is it?' he quailed.

"A deep, rough voice loudly demanded, 'Who's in there?'

---

* From *The New Path* by Swami Kriyananda.

44

"'J-Jean.'

"'Who?'

"'Jean Haupt.' By now Jean was thoroughly frightened.

"'I don't want you. I want Don Walters!' Whoever or whatever it was stormed noisily out of the building.

"Shortly after that, it must have been, when my own strange experience began.

"'Come!' As I called out, the floor beneath me began to heave in wave-like movements. An instant later I found myself being drawn out of my body and out the window into a sort of grey mist. A peculiar aspect of *Aum*, not at all pleasant, resounded loudly all around me. This was evidently not going to be a spiritually uplifting experience! Discrimination, however, was not my strong point that night.

"'How interesting!' I thought, going along with events to see where they led.

"Presently, some powerful force pitted itself against me; it seemed determined to rob me of my conscious awareness. I struggled to resist, but the opposing will was strong; I wasn't at all sure I would win. I quickly decided I'd better stop playing such a risky game.

"'Master!' I cried, urgently.

"Instantly the experience ended. The sound ceased. Back again in my body, I sat up in bed, fully awake.

"Later that day I asked Master if this had been a true experience.

"'Yes, it was. Such things sometimes happen on the path.' He added, 'Don't be afraid of them.'"

Dream-Willingness

Swami Kriyananda struggled to write one of his first books, *Crises in Modern Thought* (later retitled *Out of the Labyrinth*). Years later, he shared the story of that struggle in chapter 41 of the first edition of his autobiography, *The Path*.

"Reassurance came to me in the form of a vision. First came an ordinary dream, in which I was discussing my proposed opus with a few friends. 'To write a book of this sort,' I exclaimed, 'one would have to be willing for every bone in his body to be broken!' Then, with deep fervor, I cried, 'And I *am* willing!' The moment I said this, a great surge of energy shot up my spine. I was thrown first into wakefulness, and thence into superconsciousness. An open book, which I recognized as the book I intended to write, appeared before me. My dream-willingness that every bone in my body be broken referred, I later understood, to my need for complete mental openness—even if, in the process, it meant breaking my every single preconception. Only by such intellectual sincerity could one be worthy of writing such a book. In other words, I would have to approach with a completely open and fair mind views against which all my own nature, training, and convictions militated."

A Flying Dream

"Many years ago I had a dream in which I was flying. In the midst of this dream, I began to wonder whether I was really flying or if this was just a dream. I said to myself: 'Well, this is a strange thing to be doing! I must be dreaming.'

"So I tried to reason it out as to whether I was dreaming or awake, and I finally came to the completely logical conclusion that, in fact, I was awake. I was only doing something unusual. How surprised I was, after being so convinced in my mind of the reality of the dream, to awaken moments later and find that my flying was only a dream!

"This world, which seems so real to our logical minds, so real to our senses, so real to all the reasoning we can apply, and so coherent in that we always seem to wake up to the same dream of 'reality' when we emerge from sleep—yet when we truly wake up in superconsciousness, we see it was all a dream."

Thus the great yogis caution us to introspect how very convinced we are that life is real, when in its deepest reality, it too is a part of the cosmic dream. When we awaken to superconsciousness, the yogis say, we'll be surprised to see how certain we were that it was real—when it too was, in truth, only an illusive seeming, only a dream.

In this chapter we could have offered many more examples of important or life-changing dreams that famous people throughout history have experienced. The ones we chose are but a small sample.

In dreaming, through the ages, our souls begin to experience more fully our divine creative abilities. As we evolve spiritually, we begin finally to understand the full and magnificent implications of this Godlike ability. As Jesus says in John 10:34, "Is it not written in the scriptures, 'You, too, are gods?'"

A Few More Important Dreams

While talking with friends while writing this book, a few of them shared their recollections of a "very important or life-changing dream." Some of these dreams were so outstanding that I felt compelled to include them in this chapter.

"Who Is Steering the Ship?"

One friend, who at the time had heavy responsibilities in guiding a large community through a difficult challenge, shared this dream: "I was the captain of a big clipper ship with huge sails and a large group as crew and passengers, all of whom were my responsibility. For a while, the weather was beautiful and we had smooth sailing. Then a violent storm arose. Frantically I clutched the wheel and tried to control the ship, but it looked as though we were being blown badly off course, perhaps onto deadly rocks that would destroy the ship and take our lives. At the height of the storm, I cried out to God for help. At that moment, I was pulled out of my body in a way that allowed me to be some distance from the ship and to be able to observe the ship and the storm in an unusual way. I witnessed the whole scene as a cross section of sea and sky. And the ship, instead of being steered by me, was attached to a cable under the ocean that moved the vessel along a defined track. All of my frantic steering was absolutely fruitless. The ship was being steered by forces that had nothing to do with my efforts. I could see that it would safely reach its destination with little or no help from me. The dream taught me that it was not I, but God, who was in charge. I knew this in theory, but the dream reinforced it in a powerful way."

"My Mom in a Rickshaw"

"Twenty years ago my mother was diagnosed with severe leukemia. After a time of treatment and a brief remission, the doctors told us that there was little hope for her. But I said: 'By my will, I'm going to pray harder and harder and make her well!' At this time, I had a dream in which my mother was riding in the back of a little bicycle rickshaw that I was peddling slowly and laboriously uphill. The hill was *really* steep and I was peddling as hard as I could, just trying and trying. Finally, my mom leaped out of the back of the rickshaw and said to me: 'Oh honey, you don't need to try so hard.' Saying that, she turned and *ran* up the hill, filled with joy and light. She died a few weeks later in a state of great bliss. My dream taught me that [God] was taking care of Mom better than I could ever do by my effort alone. It wasn't up to *me* to make her well. My prayer efforts were good, yes! But not with tension and struggle—rather with a sense of joyful participation with the Divine Mother of the universe."

"Who Is Cleaning Up My Karma?"

"In my dream, I came upon a large pile of garbage. *Really* large,

48

looming over me like a small mountain. A shovel appeared in my hand and I knew that this pile represented my past karma and that it was time for me to clean it up. So I set to the task. Very soon I realized that my efforts, one shovel-full at time, were making very little impact on the giant pile. I saw that at this rate, it would take me forever to clean it up! Finally, after much more shoveling, I gave up and sat down to meditate and to pray for help. As I became quiet, I could hear the sound of a giant machine, working out of sight, over on the other side of the garbage pile. Because I am familiar with large machinery, I could tell from the sound it was making that it was a backhoe. Making my way around the pile to investigate the pile, I found that indeed a backhoe was attacking the karma pile with great speed and success. In the driver's seat was Master [Paramhansa Yogananda]! And he was smiling at me. What a relief to see the help, unbeknownst to me, which I had been receiving all along. But then I understood that I couldn't sit back and watch him do all the work. I needed to pick up my little shovel and keep going. My dream reminded me of the formula Yogananda gives us for how much spiritual help we are offered: 25 percent is our own effort, 25 percent is the effort of the guru on our behalf, and 50 percent is the grace of God. Master is also quick to remind us that our own 25 percent must never be neglected."

"Why Do I Keep Having This Same Dream?"

"For many nights I kept having the same dream. In the dream I saw a large house and loved it! I wanted to own and live in this house very much. I would go inside the house and try to think of ways I could possess it. But there was one big problem. The basement of the house was full of trash. I knew it had to be cleaned out in order for me to be able to move into the house. I would then begin cleaning it up, but could never finish the job before I woke up. This dream recurred for many months. I kept trying to figure out what it could possibly mean. I thought perhaps that my husband

and I needed to buy a house to live in and that we should start looking for just the right one. After several more repetitions, as in the dream I was starting the cleaning-the-basement process, a friend appeared and said he would help me. This friend represents to me the epitome of meditation in that he is a *very* strong and faithful meditator. This time, when I awoke, I knew that the house did not represent my desire for a house to live in; it represented my mind. The basement was my subconscious and it was full of old memories, habits, and attachments which needed to be cleaned up; but I was going about it the wrong way, trying to clean it out piece by piece. Meditation was and is a better and faster solution to letting go of one's old subconscious trash."

"It Saved My Life"

"When I was twenty-nine and a single mom with a two-year-old daughter, I was diagnosed with stage-four uterine cancer. Although I was going through chemotherapy and all the usual procedures to save my life, the prognosis was not good. In fact I had a 5 percent chance of surviving! Nevertheless, I was determined to live and to raise my daughter, and I pursued every possible means of healing. In the midst of this I had a dream which, I believe, saved my life. In the dream, aliens landed in a silver saucer spaceship. They approached me and told me that what I needed was called "INTERFERON," and then they handed me some. I had no idea what "interferon" was! But the message was so clear and the word so distinct. I had worked with dreams enough to recognize that aliens can serve as a metaphor for information coming from above and beyond. Because the message was so vivid and specific, I told my doctor about the dream. He was silent for a moment, and then he told me that interferon was a new type of treatment that was currently being tested. He was impressed that I had dreamed this unusual and specific word, and on that basis he wrote me a prescription for interferon, which acts to boost the white blood cells in the immune system. This was one of several very specific healing dreams I had that directed me in my process of full and complete healing from fourth-stage cancer. (The cancer went into full remission and remains that way to this day eighteen years later). I am convinced that these were divine messages and that my healing was a miracle of God's grace. To this day I am grateful to be alive."

Savitri's Astral World Dream

To conclude this chapter I would like to offer an account of a wonderful dream of my own. Perhaps it seems a little odd that I should recount my own dream recollections in this chapter, to stand beside the dreams of great ones like Yogananda, Swami Kriyananda, Abraham Lincoln, and biblical prophets. I do so in order to illustrate the fact that whoever you are, whatever your station in life, spiritually important and life-changing dreams can come to you.

Most people probably have thousands of dreams over the course of a lifetime. I am one of those people who, for better or for worse, have an extremely active dream-life, which I typically remember upon awakening. Often, as I have told my husband about "a dream I had last night," he would shake his head in amazement at the full-length movie quality of my dreams, which are huge, vivid, and lengthy productions in full color and surround-sound.

As vivid as many of them may be, most of my dreams fall in the more common category of subconscious meanderings through the stored memories of a busy life. Only rarely have I had dreams of a more superconscious nature, when I dreamt of a saint or a master and was blessed by their presence. Would that there were more of those! I assume they will appear when my spiritual life is more developed.

But then, in February 2006, I experienced an unexpected and amazing dream—the most remarkable dream I ever had! I think I would have to classify it as "superconscious," because of its qualities of light, upliftment, and the major lessons I learned from it. And I suspect the lessons in my dream are ones we all need to learn.

The dream was very long, or at least when I awoke, I felt it had been going on for a long time. And there were several sections or components to it.

It began as I became aware that I was on some sort of transportation system, like the small electric train-shuttles you find in some airports, which take you from one terminal to another. I was traveling with a few people; we were all standing in the shuttle, quietly, not relating to each other, feeling sort of dazed while the shuttle took us "somewhere." I then realized with certainty that I had died and was being taken to a heavenly or astral world. I felt no alarm or strangeness. Rather, it seemed quite natural.

At our destination the shuttle stopped, the doors pulled back, and we emerged. There were many people there to meet us. I didn't recognize anyone, but I felt sweet and welcoming vibrations. Again, everything seemed natural and right—except that I felt a little dazed and tired, though still looking forward to what would happen next.

A very kind-looking woman approached; I didn't know who she was, but I felt at home with her—as if she were a fellow truth-seeker I was meeting for the first time. I knew she had been "assigned" to help me. She took me to a rejuvenation area. From here on in the dream, I visited different areas, which were called "lokas."* Throughout the long dream I was aware of being in the astral realms, and enjoying it very much! The vibrations were soothing and the scenery was lovely everywhere I went.

Loka #1: In this first rejuvenation loka, my guide kindly explained that I was a bit "damaged" from my transition from the earth-plane and needed to revitalize my energy patterns. So we

---

* In Sanskrit the word "loka" means location or world. One fairly well known loka (to those familiar with Yogananda's teachings) is *Hiranyaloka*, the astral planet where Yogananda's guru, Sri Yukteswar, presently resides and serves.

spent some time in a heavenly spa, where I was given energy showers and soaks and other sorts of nourishing treatments. At the close of the "energy spa treatment," I could feel that I had become much stronger and more energetic, awake, and aware of my surroundings. I knew I would now be able to move about and function on my own without a guide. Beforehand, I had felt "log-gy" and my surroundings were somewhat veiled to my vision.

Before I went on to the next loka, I paused to look in a full-length mirror. I did this with a little trepidation, perhaps from the memory of what my old physical body had looked like before I had made my recent transition, and perhaps from the fear of not knowing how my astral body would appear. In the mirror I simply saw myself. It was obviously me—no question about that, but now I saw reflected a beautiful and much younger me. I wore a long shimmering gown of aqua-blue. My hair was wavy and golden-brown, and fell below my shoulders. I didn't stay long at the mirror, but I had the notion that if I didn't like this particular appearance, I could probably, with some energy on my part, change it into anything I wished (for example, for a brief moment I considered making my hair longer). I decided that I could do that later if it seemed appropriate. There was much to be explored in my new habitat, and I was excited to get on with my adventures.

Loka #2: I found myself visiting a small home. It was a beautiful, Japanese-type house, full of white light, highly polished floors, and sliding screens. Here I saw a man and woman I know well, who love children very much. (This was the first time in the dream I recognized anybody from my present life.) With the couple were three beautiful young children who were playing and shouting with childish glee and running from room to room while the couple laughingly tried to keep up with them. I knew that these people were fulfilling, in the astral world, dreams they had not been able to manifest fully in their last lifetime. I didn't want to stay (it was not the sort of astral world I had in mind for myself), so I said a friendly hello to all and backed out of the room. At that point, the woman came to say good-bye and to see me out. As I looked into her eyes, a message was strongly conveyed to me—a combination of joy and satisfaction at being where she was mingled with a sadness that she was somewhat stuck there and couldn't join in my explorations.

Loka #3: Next I visited a small, narrow, high-ceilinged room, full of shadows and darkness, but not unpleasant or frightening. Here were four or five men who I understood had been famous rock stars in their last life on earth. They were friendly and welcoming. I was not really sure exactly who they were. There was pleasant music in the background, not at all the sort of music they had played and sung on earth. One of them took me aside to show me an item very important to him. It was a box—sort of like a child's Jack-in-the-box. He carefully and lovingly opened it. I saw inside a small stuffed animal. In the center of its chest something peaked out from inside its stuffing, like a beating heart or a light.

Then I noticed that all the men had similar boxes, each with a different childhood toy or memento inside, each of which was very dear to him personally. I knew, without anybody saying anything, that these items represented "the joy of a sweet childhood memory." Somehow these toys were bringing the rock stars great comfort and helping them overcome a lack in their emotional natures. I was glad for them, but also glad not to have to stay in this loka, for they seemed a little sad and immobile.

Loka #4: I was then asked to go on a river trip with a young woman who was piloting a small cabin-cruiser boat. We were standing in the bow, heading up a beautiful river. She was beside me steering, and I could feel the wind in my hair. I didn't know her, but I was grateful that she had invited me on the trip, because it was indescribably beautiful. The river was smooth and shining with light. It kept changing colors around every bend—manifesting all the colors of the rainbow. The river wound through tall canyons, like the Grand Canyon, and these too kept changing colors. It was magnificent! I thoroughly enjoyed every minute of this expedition!

After traveling upstream for a while amidst all this amazing astral beauty, my hostess suggested that we stop at a guesthouse for some refreshments. Inside the charming riverside house were two more unknown but very friendly ladies, who gave me a soft drink. As we stood there enjoying our beverages, I noticed that they began to seem very disturbed, looking anxiously toward the front doors of the guesthouse. They slowly backed up against a wall, holding their drinks on top of their heads. I was mystified by their behavior, but when I looked toward the front doors, which were partially open, I could see small shadowy figures dashing back and forth in front of the door and windows. I recognized that my hostesses were frightened of these beings and were trying to move farther away from the door to protect themselves.

I realized I was becoming a little frightened too at what might be out there, so I moved over to stand near where the hostesses were cowering and also to put my drink on top of my head ("When in Rome . . ."). Feeling silly about my actions, I then said, "Well, let's do something positive. Let's chant!" (Somehow, I had taken one of my earthly mottos along with me into the astral world: "When in doubt, chant!") So I started chanting "Jai Guru," and the hostesses joined me.

Suddenly then, behind our chanting voices, I began to hear Swami Kriyananda's voice singing one of his beautiful original songs. I *wish* I could recall which song it was, but that knowledge has slipped away. As I was chanting and listening to his voice simultaneously, the words of Swami's song began to change. We stopped chanting to listen more carefully. The lyrics were not the familiar words I knew, though they still went along perfectly with the melody. Swami's voice was now singing specific words of instruction about what was going on regarding the frightening entities outside the doorway.

He sang these words to us: "Do not fear them! They are just harmless lower astral entities. They saw you in here enjoying your drinks and simply wanted to enter and take part; but they were afraid to do so, acting a bit like shy children, running about and peeking inside. All will be well if you welcome them in to join you in your refreshments." And so we did, and all was well.

I continued to wander and enjoy the beautiful astral lands, but I have no further specific memories, except that of much time passing in enjoyment of the beauty and peace. Then someone came to me and said: "Devi [a close friend of mine] is arriving at the shuttle station. Would you like to go and greet her?" Well, of course, I was delighted and rushed to the place where I myself had arrived a while back. I thought that I could help her get oriented, or take her to the "energy spa" for her arrival treatment, or to see a rainbow waterfall or something.

At the terminus I saw exactly the same scene there, as when I had arrived. The shuttle pulled in with people standing on it; the doors slid back, and they walked off. They seemed in the same condition I had been in when I arrived, a little dazed and unaware of what to do or what was going on. Friendly guides were on hand to help them.

And then I saw Devi. She stepped off the shuttle, and it was immediately evident to me that she was not at all dazed or un-aware. She knew exactly where she was. She paused for just a moment and looked straight at me, very calmly but with great intensity. She didn't say a word, but I clearly "heard" what she wanted to communicate: "Savitri, what are you doing here? You are wasting time enjoying the beauties of this astral world. Why do that? Don't you know there is so much *more?*" With that, and not another glance in my direction, she moved off into the dis-tance. I knew she was moving on to a much higher loka, perhaps even to full God-realization.

I was astonished and impressed. Many things became clear in

that moment. I realized that in this astral world I had not seen those whom I should have been seeking, the saints and masters. I had not been meditating. I had not been praying or inwardly communing with the Highest. True, Swamiji had come to me briefly in the form of his music, in order to give me instruction in a time of need—and that was a very good lesson in itself—but that was all. Where was Master; where were all my gurus? Where was Swami? Where was my husband Sudarshan, or any others of my Ananda family? Why had I not seen them here? Either they were not here yet, or they had acted like Devi and gone on immediately to a higher *loka*. I was just as stuck as the family with their children, or the rock stars with their childhood toys.

True, this astral planet was surpassingly lovely and satisfying to my love of nature, beauty, calmness, and harmony. I had been enjoying myself immensely. But now I saw that I had been lulled into apathy by it all and had forgotten my goal. The "traps of beauty," as Yogananda described them, had pulled me in and held me for a time. So I sat down right where I was and began to pray and meditate.

And then I woke up.

The lessons I learned from this dream are: First, what a great blessing it is to have spiritual friends with the courage to let you know when you have taken a sidetrack on your path.

Paramhansa Yogananda said that those who meditate will, to varying degrees after their passing, be aware of their time in the astral world and not sleep or dream through those intervals between incarnations as many people do. I can imagine how enthralled we could become in the beauties of a very special astral paradise. But as lovely, restful, and satisfying as we may find it, it will eventually lose its attraction. (*Yawn.* "So there's yet another rainbow river canyon. Big deal!")

In whatever loka we find ourselves, we should *never* delay our soul's journey to freedom in God. If we find ourselves in paradise (on earth or in heaven), we need to keep our consciousness dynamic and ever pointed toward the goal. We should never postpone or give in to apathy; rather we should do whatever it takes to hurry us toward our destiny of true wakefulness in God-realization.

Chapter Four

Where Do Our Dreams Come From?

In waking, eating, working, dreaming, sleeping,

Serving, meditating, chanting, divinely loving,

My soul will constantly hum, unheard by any:

God! God! God!

—from the poem "God! God! God!" by Paramhansa Yogananda, *Whispers from Eternity* (2008 edition, edited by Swami Kriyananda)

Three Levels of Consciousness

According to Paramhansa Yogananda, there is no such thing as "unconsciousness." The universal consciousness, or God, has produced everything in existence, and is also a part of everything in existence. Everyone and everything, even the rocks, has consciousness. Granted there is only a low awareness of consciousness in the rocks and minerals—still a germ of consciousness exists in every atom.

In sleep we are not unconscious. One indication this is true is that, upon awakening, we can feel how well or how badly we slept. Even death itself does not produce an unconscious state. Yoga philosophy describes death as a doorway into a different dimension and a new state of consciousness. We have never been unconscious, nor will we ever be unconscious.

Yogananda explained this concept in one of his early *Yogoda Lessons* (1930): "Human consciousness is never wholly suspended. During the dream state, the ego is semi-unconscious of the world and of the sense experiences—yet it is conscious of the dream world. It is also conscious of deep sleep while in that state. The link between consciousness and subconsciousness is unbroken; otherwise dreams could not be recalled when consciousness is fully resumed. It is impossible to be wholly unconscious; the soul's subjective consciousness (the ego) may be asleep or resting, but this can never be termed 'unconsciousness.'"

The totality of a human being's consciousness, generally speaking, is composed of three levels: not only the familiar levels of consciousness and subconsciousness, but also the superconsciousness of which Yogananda speaks extensively. These levels of consciousness represent differing degrees of awareness and energy.

Subconsciousness

Subconsciousness is a relatively dim level of awareness most commonly experienced during the lowered-energy level of nightly sleep. Popularized in modern times by Sigmund Freud, the subconscious is the hidden but sometimes dominant part of our psyche. We may think of it as the repository of all remembered experiences, impressions left on the mind by those experiences, and tendencies awakened or reinforced by those impressions. Every experience we've ever had, every thought, every impression of loss or gain, resides in the subconscious mind and determines our patterns of thought and behavior far more than we realize. When we dream at night, we are operating primarily on the subconscious level.

All day long, while conscious, we are receiving input through the five senses: seeing, hearing, touching, smelling, and tasting.

The input gathered by the senses is stored in the form of memories in the subconscious. At night or when we are asleep, the conscious mind goes dormant and the subconscious mind takes charge. The memories and impressions of the previous day or from our past are resurrected, resorted, and played back to us in the form of dreams.

The subconscious mind is always awake; it works through memory while consciousness predominates, runs the "motion picture theater of dreamland" while in the dream-sleep state, and enjoys some serenity during the deepest states of sleep or in deep meditation.

In our active hours, the subconscious mind influences our behavior, our very attitudes toward life. The subconscious mind influences the intellect by prompting it with deep-seated feelings, habit patterns, and personal tendencies. (Our conscious decisions are never as independent as we like to believe them!) Harmful habits, though difficult to banish from the mind, can—by repeated, *conscious* effort—be redirected into positive channels.

The subconscious mind is like the vast ocean with its floor of mountains, valleys, and broad plains. Conscious awareness protrudes from this ocean like a little island. Invisible to the island dwellers is the great underwater region around them; the innumerable habits, tendencies, and unformed impressions that underlie the conscious mind. They represent a dimmer, but nonetheless very real, part of our total awareness.

The Conscious Mind

The conscious mind is our normal waking state of awareness. But it represents only a small part of our total consciousness. A far larger part of it lies in subconsciousness. The conscious state offers us rational awareness, which ordinarily guides our daily, waking lives. When we receive input from the five senses, analyze the facts, and base our actions on this information, we are using the conscious level of our minds. We make decisions and solve problems primarily with the conscious mind. The conscious mind, dependent on the intellect, seeks reasonable solutions to its problems.

During waking hours, the conscious state is predominant, with the subconscious and superconscious states trailing behind. We generally stay on the plane of physical consciousness while awake, but when we are forcibly (through drugs or injury) or passively (through fatigue) led into the subconscious chamber of dreams and deepest sleep, the ego becomes only dimly conscious of itself.

The ordinary ego can support only one state at a time: the physically conscious state, the subconscious state, or the deepest state of sleep, which Yogananda calls semi-superconsciousness. Only a "master"—one who has *mastered* himself on every level—can dwell in constant superconsciousness, maintaining that state at all times.

Superconsciousness

Between the conscious and subconscious minds, dividing but also uniting them, is the third level of awareness: the superconscious. Though the state of superconsciousness is latent in every individual, it is largely unrealized in most people. When we connect with superconsciousness, we become aware of our interconnection with all people and all of life. In superconsciousness our intuitive guidance is flawless, and we can effortlessly perceive the essence of any problem and the appropriate solution for that problem.

Superconsciousness represents a much higher degree of awareness than the conscious and subconscious minds. Indeed, it is the true source of all awareness. The conscious and subconscious minds filter that higher awareness—merely stepping it down, so to speak, as a transformer converts a high voltage to a lower one and makes it available to our homes.

Superconsciousness may be compared to the infinite sky overhead, with its vast panoply of stars. We know that the stars are always there, shining. We can only see them, however, when the sunlight doesn't fill the sky and obscure them. The sunlight, in this analogy, represents ego-generated thoughts and feelings, which blot out superconscious awareness from our mental sky. That superconsciousness is always with us, however. It is simply not dynamic to our normal waking consciousness.

Superconsciousness is situated, as the name implies, above our normal state of wakefulness. From that higher level come our occasional deep insights and inspirations, when our minds are in a calm and uplifted state. Those insights may penetrate the light of ego-wakefulness like brilliant comets, which can sometimes be seen in the sky even in bright daylight.

Superconsciousness is the realm of true visions. It contains the ecstasy experienced during periods of deep meditation, intense prayer, or inward upliftment, when the ego's restlessness has been temporarily stilled.

Superconscious Dreams or Visions

Occasionally we are able to have a superconscious dream, which comes to us through a higher state of consciousness—that is, through the Higher Self or God. These dreams can offer us perfect guidance or deep inspiration. The more we live a spiritually-oriented life focused on prayer and meditation, a life which increases our awareness of superconsciousness, the more likely we are to experience this sort of dream. But for the most part, our ordinary dreams emerge from the subconscious.

Yogananda says: "During retirement to the subconscious dream chamber, consciousness casts off its garment of the gross sensations of touch, smell, taste, sight, and audition. But though divested of its physical sense instruments of perception, consciousness still retains its intuitive powers of cognition through the subconscious, and beholds the dreams resulting from memories, thoughts, and the activity of the subtle senses. However, when the ego enters the silent chambers of deep sleep (semi-superconsciousness) its experiences consist of the unalloyed enjoyment of real peace. The human consciousness, turned within, here begins to resume its normal state of calmness, peace, and joy. The conscious state is marked by restlessness; the subconscious state, by a mixture of restfulness and activity; but bliss reigns in the superconscious state. The great yoga masters have complete control over all forms of consciousness, and can remain in one or more of these states at will."

Dreaming and the Three Bodies

Another way of looking at the "location" or origin point of dreams is through understanding the three bodies we possess: the physical body, the astral body, and the causal body. When we are dreaming we are operating more from the astral realm, a state (or "body") in which imagination, visualization, and the willful manipulation of energy are more dominant. The physical, astral, and causal bodies and realms are explained more fully by Sri Yukteswar, Yogananda's guru, in *Autobiography of a Yogi* in the fascinating chapter called "The Resurrection of Sri Yukteswar." Here is a short excerpt from that chapter:

"The interpenetration of man's three bodies is expressed in many ways through his threefold nature. In the wakeful state on earth a human being is conscious more or less of his three vehicles. When he is sensuously intent on tasting, smelling, touching, listening, or seeing, he is working principally through his physical body. Visualizing or willing, he is working mainly through his astral body. His causal medium finds expression when man is thinking or diving deep in introspection or meditation; the cosmical thoughts of genius come to the man who habitually contacts his causal body. In this sense an individual may be classified broadly as 'a material man,' 'an energetic man,' or 'an intellectual man.'

"A man identifies himself about sixteen hours daily with his physical vehicle. Then he sleeps; if he dreams, he remains in his astral body, effortlessly creating any object . . . . If man's sleep be deep and dreamless, for several hours he is able to transfer his consciousness, or sense of I-ness, to the causal body; such sleep is revivifying. A dreamer is contacting his astral and not his causal body; his sleep is not fully refreshing."

To summarize: In meditation, we strive to go beyond thought. As long as we are busy thinking, we are in the conscious plane, identified primarily with our material bodies. When we sleep and dream, we are on the subconscious plane, and in our astral bodies. And when our minds are fully withdrawn into a superconscious state, they become centered in our ideational, or causal, bodies.

Most dreams are like movies, emanating from the projection booth of our subconscious minds. They are made of energy and contain light, sound, color, sensations, and emotions of all sorts. Rarely, when we are dreaming, are we aware that we are dreaming. And yet most dreams seem to have a "dreamlike" quality to them. Granted we may experience vivid dreams or even gripping nightmares, which linger on in their emotional impact long after we awaken. But for most people, dreams are very "dreamlike" and fade from the conscious mind quickly. Do they have a purpose? We seem to spend a sizable chunk of our lives in the dream state. Why?

The next chapter contains an explanation of why we dream and the true meaning of dreaming.

Chapter Five

Why Do We Dream?

Life is a dream,

Time like a stream,

Carries our burdens away.

—from *Songs of Divine Joy* by Swami Kriyananda

Never go to bed at night until you have convinced your mind that this world is God's dream.

—Paramhansa Yogananda, as quoted by Swami Kriyananda in *The New Path*

In a future chapter we will discuss the content of our dreams (dream interpretations and analysis), including the elements and symbols of our dreams and what they might mean to us. But now we will address the central question of *why* we dream and the true meaning of dreaming.

As stated earlier, there are many theories as to why we dream. However, in the huge body of information about dreams and dreaming, rarely, if ever, does any scholar or scientist dare give a definitive opinion on why we dream. They say, "We simply don't know for sure." But Paramhansa Yogananda *did* dare to say: "I know exactly both why and how we dream." He could say this with full authority, because he was (is!) a fully Self-realized Master, having firsthand experience of all levels of consciousness—especially superconsciousness, in which all knowledge has its ultimate existence.

The Magic Shadow-Show

There are many dreamlike aspects of life. Often we can't remember exactly what happened yesterday, or even what we were thinking five minutes ago—it sort of comes and goes, like forms appearing out of the mists and disappearing again. Centuries ago, "magic shadow-shows" were a popular form of entertainment. From candlelight in a box, moving shadows were projected onto a screen, creating an illusion of reality.

The "shadow-show" of modern times is the cinema. The images on the movie screen, also, are true to the sense of sight—far more so than in shadow-shows. To this illusion has now been added the dimension of sound.

In this world, similarly, appearances are projected onto the screen of space by the sun and by subtle electrical currents. Life itself, as all the great yogis declare, is an illusion: the most convincing show of all! It is presented to us three-dimensionally. And it includes the illusion of other senses as well: smell, taste, and touch. Life, however, for all its persuasiveness, is as fundamentally unreal as any magic shadow-show.

This is an ancient concept, most notably taught in India: that the whole universe is *maya*, a cosmic illusion. *Maya* is a Sanskrit word meaning, literally, "magical measurer," or that which pretends to measure the Immeasurable and divide it into opposites.

The yoga scriptures contain frequent references to this teaching. An image they often employ to illustrate the concept of *maya* is that of dreaming. For just as dreams vanish when we wake, so does manifested existence vanish before our gaze when we waken in supreme wisdom. In the dream state we can create whatever we fancy in our minds: people, stars, galaxies—anything. God, similarly, in His dream of creation, manifests the universe.

Life Is a Dream

Life, even for ordinary human beings, possesses a certain dreamlike quality. People often make such remarks as, "I can't believe this is happening to me," or, "This whole day seems unbelievable!" On some deeper level of our consciousness, this world, which seems so real most of the time, may also, at certain times, feel very unreal. We all know, from our own experiences, that things happen which make us ask the question, "Am I dreaming? Perhaps I should I pinch my arm to wake myself up!"

Nevertheless, when awake, we generally are convinced of the reality of the world around us, because the cosmic spectacle, unlike our subconscious dreams, is self-consistent. We awaken daily to the same "scenario."

Life exerts a further persuasion: the fact that we ourselves are part of the cosmic dream. In sleep we create our own dreams, but our influence within the cosmic dream is minimal. For it was God who brought this dream into being out of cosmic consciousness. God-tuned sages have declared from personal experience—and modern physicists have made similar statements—that the cosmos exists only in consciousness, not as an objective fact.

Another reason this cosmic dream seems truer than our own nightly dreams is its intense vividness. The cosmic illusion was created in superconsciousness; it lacks the vague, slightly irrational quality of human dreams.

Yogananda illustrated this point with a story: A king was sleeping on a bed of gold and dreaming that he was very poor. He cried in his sleep, begging for a penny. The queen, hearing him cry out, shook him from his nightmare. She asked, "What is the matter with you? Don't you know you are a king? Why are you crying and begging?"

The king awoke, saying, "Oh, oh, I must have been dreaming. I dreamed I was poor and starving."

When the king was dreaming he was poor, you couldn't convince him he was a wealthy king. So it is with us. In the deepest sleep states, our souls are temporarily free. We have no bodies, no country, no name, no sex, nothing! But as soon as we wake, how could we be convinced that we are not our bodies? As soon as a little pain comes, we cry. So the pure soul becomes ego-ruled during the daytime. In other words, the soul ascribes all the conditions of the body to itself, and we call that the ego. The ego is the soul identified with the body.

The True Purpose of Our Dreams

Yogananda says, very simply, that the purpose of dreaming is to instruct and entertain us. This also, he says, is the purpose of life in general. When we progress spiritually, we come to understand that life is also a dream. More specifically, the most important and instructive aspect of dreaming in general is to teach us that *all of life is a dream.*

One of the major themes of Yogananda's teachings is the importance of cognizing the dream nature of the universe. He explains, as many other great yoga masters have explained through the centuries, that the way we dream mimics the mechanism which produces all of life, as we perceive it. Our life, our world, and all we know are like movies, or plays of light and shadow projected on the screen of space. Our nightly dreams are little "movies" within the big movie of life.

Dreams come to us to strongly hint that what we call reality or life is not as solid and real as it may seem. *This, according to the deeper teachings of yoga, is the primary reason we dream!* Other reasons offered as theories for why we dream may have some validity, but they are not nearly as important as this one central concept: we dream to help us understand a fundamental reality: Life itself is a dream.

Energy, Will Power, and Dreams

It is important to understand the element of energy in dreams. Creative energy combined with our imagination produces dreams. Energy has the power to materialize our thoughts, just as God's thoughts combined with energy materialized this universe. Through this creative process God shows us that if we have control over energy we can create, just as He does. Behind all of nature is the Cosmic Intelligence, plus energy. Energy is the missing link between matter and consciousness. Energy and consciousness are a part of everything. Likewise, God shows us that in our "dreamland theaters," we can create a replica of this dream world, provided we have consciousness and energy under our control through our will power.

The Phenomena of Dreams

Most people dream at night, but few take their jumbled dreams seriously. So we often say that an essential lesson dreamland has to offer is that we must not take our earthly experiences too seriously either, for they are nothing but a series of vast dream movies shown to entertain us. Yogananda explains: "The Heavenly Father meant to entertain and educate us, His immortal children, with a variety of earthly movies. We must behold comedies, tragedies, and newsreels of life movies with an entertained joyous attitude, and learn from them without being overcome by their emotional impact."

In dreamland we often forget our names, bodies, nationalities, possessions, and all our frailties. Similarly, we must always be aware that the soul is not permanently attached to its present bodily temple, its environment, family, sex, or race.

God gave the soul and mind the power to materialize thoughts in dreamland and create a miniature cosmos, even as God does. The Creator froze all thoughts into substance, and we perceive the dream of the Cosmos with its various sensations. God shows that we, being His divine children, can create even as He does. The phenomena of dreams show us that the mind can reproduce an exact copy of our worldly experiences and material life.

In dreamland our spirit (or soul) becomes free to create a cosmos after its own fancy. It can move in a new body, in a new world; enjoy ice cream or hot tea; live in the hot desert of the Sahara, or in the bleak regions of Alaska, or the heights of the Himalayas. In dreamland the soul can masquerade as a poor man or a king; it can satisfy all its unfulfilled earthly desires by materializing them into dream experiences. Through dreams we can create, if we will, a perfect world, free from poverty, sickness, wickedness, and ignorance. In dreams we can be a part of anything that does not seem possible in earthly life. Here we can perceive the birth of a baby or the death of a man. Here we can cry or smile, hear songs, smell flowers, touch, feel, think, reason, meditate, and perform every activity of earthly life.

What Is Reality?

Just as we find this variety-filled dream life interesting, without believing in its actuality, so we must prove ourselves to be God's immortal children, who can learn and be entertained by the "cosmic movies" of life without forgetting that they are temporary and delusive. We must prove ourselves to be true sons and daughters of God by appreciating the lessons of these "cosmic movies," and without losing the unchangeable, joyous poise of our inner being—the true reflections of immortal, unchangeable God.

The following is a story Yogananda often told to illustrate the principles outlined above.

"There was a farmer standing by a tree, absorbed in thought. His wife came rushing up, weeping, to announce that their only son had just been killed a cobra. The farmer made no reply. Stunned by his seeming indifference, the wife cried, 'You are heartless!'

"'You don't understand,' the farmer replied. 'Last night I dreamed that I was a king, and that I had seven sons. They went out into the forest and all were bitten by cobras and died. Now I am wondering whether I ought to weep for my seven dead sons in that dream, or for our one son who has just been killed in this dream we are dreaming now.'

"The farmer was a man of spiritual vision. To him, the material world and the subconscious dream-world were both equally unreal.*

When we dream at night, this present dream fades into unreality, and only that subconscious dream world seems real. When we return again to the dream of this world, that other dream is forgotten.

Everything exists only in consciousness. This does not mean that we do not have to play by the rules of this dream world. Certainly we do! The laws of gravity work even if you choose not to believe in them. If you hit your dream head with a dream hammer, it will dream hurt! But still it is all an illusion. If, at night, you dream that you bump your head against a wall, you may get an imaginary pain in your head. The moment you awake, however, you realize that there was no wall there to hurt you. The pain you experienced was in your mind, but not in your head! The same is true of this dream you are dreaming now. This isn't to say that the physical universe is not real; it does have a certain reality to it. Its reality, however, is not what it appears to be. The underlying reality of all existence is consciousness. God dreamed this whole universe into existence. This world seems real to you because God dreamed *you* into existence along with His cosmic dream. You are part of your Creator's dream.

---

* From *The Essence of Self-Realization* by Swami Kriyananda.

Paramhansa Yogananda said: "A man is sleeping, and dreams that he is a soldier. He goes into battle, fights bravely, then is fatally wounded. Sadly he dreams of his approaching death, perhaps thinking of the dear ones he must leave behind.

"Suddenly he wakes up. In joyful relief he cries, 'Ah! I am not a soldier, and I am not dying! It was only a dream.' And he laughs to find himself alive and well.

"But what of the soldier who actually fights in this earth-life, and is wounded and killed? Suddenly, in the astral world, he wakes up to find that it was all just a dream; that in that other world he has no physical body, no flesh to be wounded, no bones to be broken.

"Don't you see? All the experiences of this world are like that. They are nothing but dream experiences."*

More About the Dream Nature of the Universe

The whole cosmos is a materialized thought of the Creator. This heavy, earthly clod, floating in space, is a dream of God. He made all things out of His consciousness, even as man in his dream consciousness reproduces and vivifies a creation with its creatures.

God first created the earth as an idea. God did not have centillions of atoms to put together; really he had *nothing* to work with, except his consciousness. Therefore, in that consciousness, He thought it into existence. He visualized, dreamed, or "quickened" the thoughts into energy atoms. This is the ideational or causal form of creation. He then coordinated the atoms into energy patterns, the astral or energy form of creation, and finally into this solid sphere of the material world. Matter is, as science declares today, only energy. What gives the appearance of solidity is vibrating energy.

Swami Kriyananda often gives the example of a fan or a propeller to illustrate this point. When you look at an unmoving fan or propeller, you see the spaces between the blades. But once it is turning fast enough, it appears to be a solid disk. Energy, when moving fast enough, produces the appearance and even the sensory experience of solidity to every test of sight, smell, feeling, taste, and touch. But it is no more real than the dreams you have at might.

All the molecules of creation are held together by the will of God. When it is time for this planet to disappear, the Divine Creative Force will withdraw its will and the earth will disintegrate into energy. Energy will dissolve into consciousness; the earth-idea will disappear from objectivity.

The substance of a dream is held in materialization by the subconscious thought of the dreamer. When that cohesive thought is withdrawn in wakefulness, the dream and its elements dissolve. A man closes his eyes and erects a dream-creation, which, on awakening, he effortlessly dematerializes. He follows the divine archetypal pattern. Similarly, when he awakens in cosmic consciousness, he will be able to dematerialize effortlessly the illusions of the cosmic dream.

Many modern discoveries help man comprehend the cosmos as a varied expression of one power-light, guided by divine intelligence. The wonders of motion pictures, radio, television, radar, the photoelectric cell, the all-seeing "electric eye," and atomic energies, are all based on the electromagnetic phenomenon of light. Movies can portray any miracle. From the impressive visual standpoint, no marvel is barred to trick photography. A man's transparent body can be seen rising from his gross physical form; he can walk on the water, resurrect the dead, reverse the natural sequence of developments, and play havoc with time and space.

Similarities Between Dreams and Movies

The lifelike images of a motion picture illustrate many truths concerning creation. The Cosmic Director has written His own plays, and assembled tremendous casts for the pageant of the centuries. From the dark booth of eternity, God pours a creative beam through the films of successive ages, and the pictures are thrown on the screen of space. Just as the motion-picture images appear to be real, but are only combinations of light and shade, so is the universal variety nothing more than a "delusive seeming." The planetary spheres, with their countless forms of life, are but figures in a cosmic motion picture, temporarily true to five sense perceptions as the scenes are cast on the screen of man's consciousness by the infinite creative beam.

A cinema attendee can glance behind himself and see that all screen images are appearing through the instrumentality of one imageless beam of light. The colorful universal drama is similarly issuing from the single white light of a Cosmic Source. With inconceivable ingenuity God is staging an entertainment for his human children, making them actors as well as audience in his cosmic theater.

In a person's dream-consciousness, where he has loosened in sleep his clutch on the egoistic limitations that daily hem him round, his mind demonstrates on a nightly basis its omnipotence. There in his dream may stand a long-dead friend, the remotest continent, or resurrected scenes of childhood.

Matter appears to us as solids, liquids, gases, heat, light, electricity, and energy. It is expressed in various forms, but is not what it appears to be. Just as we can behold in a dream a mountain or an ocean, or breathe the atmosphere, or feel the heat of summer, or see sunlight or electricity lighting a city, or the energy of the aurora, or the life force surging in millions of human bodies.

With that same free and unconditioned consciousness, known to all in the phenomena of dreams, a God-tuned master has forged a never-severed link. Innocent of all personal motives, and employing the creative will bestowed on him by the Creator, a yoga master can rearrange the light atoms of the universe to satisfy the sincere need of a disciple.

For this purpose were human beings and all creation made: that all should rise up as masters over delusion, knowing our dominion over the cosmos.

When we unite our consciousness with God's, we perceive this cosmos as God's dream playing out through our minds. No one can master this realization until he experiences complete unity with God. Just as a dreamer does not know that his dream ice cream cone is made up of the different vibrations of his frozen imagination, so also the cosmic dream of matter—with its solids, liquids, gases, and electricity—is not recognized as the frozen imagination of God by anyone under the spell of cosmic delusion.

How to Overcome the Cosmic Dream-Delusion

Science has proven that matter is nothing but electromagnetic waves, or frozen light. Metaphysicians say that frozen light, in turn, is frozen God-consciousness. Through meditation upon these truths, all matter can be seen as God's dream.

The cosmic delusive dream can be overcome by ever-deeper meditation, until we rise above the consciousness of our bodies, and our conscious and subconscious minds. In meditation with closed eyes, all matter passes out of the picture; and when we firmly feel that the "real world" is one consciousness of blessed omnipresence, we no longer perceive the delusive "cosmic motion picture" as reality. When we embrace the consciousness of ever-new peace—that peace which can withstand the challenge of all tests of physical pain, and passing pleasures and sorrows—then material perceptions dissolve. Everything dissolves in the fire of meditation, in the consciousness of our ever-joyous spirit.

Yogananda told an interesting story about his childhood. As a small boy he had a recurring and terrifying dream in which a tiger attacked him, grabbing and biting his leg. His crying out during these vivid nightmares would bring his mother to his side to comfort him—and to show him that there was no tiger, that his leg was not injured, that he had been merely dreaming. The last time he had this dream, he brought things under his control and, as he put it, "jumped out of the dream." He said that even at that young age, he was able to distinguish between what was real and what was unreal, both in dreams and in "real" life. Thus, suffering could no longer touch him in the same way.

So also each of us can begin to understand life as a cosmic dream-movie, by analyzing the dream-movies we create every night while sleeping. How real these dreams sometimes feel—whether beautiful dreams or nightmares! And yet our dreams, as we realize upon awakening, are only passing illusions. So, too, is your life! Realize this truth in your mind and in your meditations. Regular meditation brings a perspective that removes all binding attachments, the primary cause of human suffering. This removal process frees us to live in the eternal bliss of our souls and in oneness with God. This is the heart of Yogananda's teachings and of the philosophy of the great masters of India. Meditate and prove these teachings to yourself. The *Bhagavad Gita* declares this magnificent truth for the benefit of the world: "Even a little practice of meditation will free one from dire fears and colossal sufferings!"

Chapter Six

How Do We Dream?

When my mind weaves dreams

With threads of memories,

Then on that magic cloth will I emboss:

God! God! God!

—from the poem "God! God! God!" by Paramhansa Yogananda in *Whispers from Eternity* (2008 edition, edited by Swami Kriyananda)

What are the mechanisms by which we dream? Paramhansa Yogananda explains how it all happens in unusual detail.

During sleep, the life force (also called *prana*, or conscious cosmic energy) retires from the periphery of the body—the five senses, muscles, and motor nerves, and partially from the inner organs, including the heart and lungs—and becomes concentrated in the brain. The energy flows are reversed in sleep, no longer moving outward from the brain to the body and further outward to the world around us. Rather, the life force becomes internalized, turning inward and upward toward the brain. Paramhansa Yogananda calls this the state of "Subconscious Sensory-Motor Relaxation." He defines dreaming as: "A subconscious state of mind when the *prana* is withdrawn from the senses and combined with the imagination, which is the visualizing ability of the conscious mind."

The brain too enjoys a period of rest and passive withdrawal from all mental activity. This is during the deepest state of sleep, or semi-superconsciousness. (Semi-superconsciousness is described in more detail later in this chapter.)

At various times during our sleep-states, the brain uses life force to create dreams—life force is made available to the brain by the prana's inward/upward flow. While we sleep our energy (prana or life force) is not needed for "outwardness," as it is when we are awake and working through the five senses. In sleep, life force becomes available to be used in what Yogananda calls the "dream-movie theater."

Yogananda also states emphatically that, while we are dreaming, we are not truly resting, for our "mental movie house" is working energetically, showing us pictures and stories composed of subconscious memories, feelings, and thoughts. Ordinary dreams do not come from outside ourselves. They are created subconsciously by our minds. (In the next chapter we will discuss extraordinary or superconscious visions, which are given by God or the Higher Self, and are not created by our subconscious minds.)

During wakefulness the conscious mind works through the five senses of sight, hearing, smell, taste, and touch—but it sleeps at night. The subconscious mind works through memory during wakefulness and through dreams at night. It is awake during the day, working in the conscious mind making records (storing memories), and it is also awake during sleep, looking after the functions of the human engine (like an old but very busy janitor), as well as acting as the manager-operator of the mental movies in dreamland.

Subconsciousness: "The Old Janitor"

What a graphic image Yogananda presents—that of the subconscious mind as a multi-tasking Old Janitor who works silently and unceasingly in the background of our lives, whether we are awake or asleep. We tend to underestimate his role as he quietly and constantly goes about his duties. Perhaps we take for granted all that he does—just as one doesn't always notice the behind the scenes staff of a large building, a theater, a movie production, or any large project.

The Janitor's duties are complex and essential to the way we function as human beings. He is not the CEO of our body/mind (the soul holds that position), and he definitely needs guidance or reprogramming from time to time. But remember that our Old Janitor may get upset if we are disrespectful or mean to him; he can throw a large monkey wrench into the smooth running of our lives. But if we recognize and respect him for all that he does, he will learn to accept the soul's lovingly offered suggestions for his (and our own) highest welfare. It is true that, although firmness, discipline, and loving leadership are often called for in working with the subconscious mind, abuse never works out well in the end.

Our dreams are produced by life force passing like a bright light through the "film" of experiences (memories) preserved in the subconscious mind. As we have said before, our subconscious mind has multiple functions. It serves as a cameraman, recording all the events of a lifetime and storing them as memories. It is also a director, taking our memories and weaving them into dream-stories or fragments. In addition the subconscious is the operator of our inner dream-movie theater. The multitasking subconscious mind is always awake; it works through memory (which never sleeps) while consciousness predominates, runs the theater of dreamland in the REM sleep state, and finally enjoys some brief rest and serenity during deep sleep (semi-superconsciousness).

Dreams are a combination of consciousness, relaxed energy, and an idea (in the form of an experience or a memory). The idea, impinged in the brain cells, is the film, the relaxed energy is the current of life-force in the brain, and the ego-consciousness is the projector. In the projection of a dream, the subconsciousness provides the darkened theater (sleep-state) and the movie screen, and the relaxed energy from the nerves gather in the brain. So when a person is dreaming, his energy has relaxed upward into the brain, specifically into the medulla oblongata section of the brain, which is the subconscious mind's primary operating chamber. The ego takes that current of energy and passes it and its ego-consciousness through the experiences in the brain cells, projecting them as subconscious dreams. In subconscious dreams the ego, plus relaxed energy, plus all of the ideas/experiences/memories being stored in the subconscious mind produce our dream images.

Dream-Movie "Credits"

I have often (laughingly) wondered if, at the end of a particularly interesting dream, I might see a list of credits for who did what in the dream-movie, rolling up the screen of my mind just like at the close of a regular movie.

Indeed, Yogananda makes it sound like this may be the case when he offers further details on the mechanism of dreaming, making graphic comparisons between dreams and movies.

Director: The subconscious mind is the coordinator and primary director of our dream movies, sorting through all our memories and impressions to create the drama.

Writer and Photographer: The intelligence of the wakeful, conscious mind is the writer and photographer of our dreams.

Cameraman: The operator of the camera of the mind is the energy (prana or life force) of the subconscious mind.

The Actors: The actors in our dreams are our thoughts, feelings, and desires.

Storage Area: Our dreams, explains Yogananda, are stored "… in groove-like shelves in the convolutions of gray matter."

Dramas and Themes: Like movies, the subjects of our inner

films are various. Some are like newsreels of events, which actually have happened or are happening to us, and some are of imaginary events. The subconscious mind can also produce comedy or nonsense pictures to delight and entertain the conscious mind.

Screen: The screen upon which the dream movie is projected is called the *ether*, which Yogananda defines as that ethereal part of one's energy body which has the vibration of space and which separates the material world from the astral world.

Audience: The audience for our dreams is the ego, which Yogananda describes as the soul identified with the body.

Nightmares

The subconscious mind, whenever it is too taxed with the fears and worries of the conscious mind, takes revenge during the state of sleep by using the concentrated energy in the brain to project a dream tragedy or nightmare on the inner screen of relaxation. In nightmares, and tragedy and fear dreams, the subconscious mind deploringly and glaringly shows the conscious mind its undesirable thoughts. The conscious mind gets to see the evil which it may only mentally or subconsciously picture. Though often uncomfortable, this sort of dream can reveal to us areas of our psyche which are in need of positive change.

The human ego generally travels in the realm of the senses during the waking state; the ego may be said to be semiconscious while dreaming, because it dimly perceives the dream pictures during their performance and can often recall them after waking. As emphasized in a previous chapter, human consciousness is never wholly suspended. During the dream state, the ego is semiconscious of the world and of sense experiences, yet it is conscious of the dream world. It is also conscious of deep, blissful sleep while in the semi-superconscious state. The link between consciousness and subconsciousness is never fully broken while we dream; otherwise dreams could not be recalled when consciousness is fully resumed.

During retirement to the subconscious "dream chamber," our consciousness casts off its garment of the gross sensations of touch, smell, taste, sight, and audition. But though divested of its physical sense instruments of perception, consciousness still retains its intuitive powers of cognition through the subconscious, and beholds the dreams resulting from memories, thoughts, and the activity of the subtle senses, the mental reflexes of the physical senses. For example, nearly everyone can recall the vivid sensation of taste in dreams of eating ice cream, hot pie, or other delicious foods.

The Characteristics of Each State of Consciousness

When the ego enters the silent chamber of deep sleep or semi-superconsciousness, its experience consists of the unalloyed enjoyment of real peace. The human consciousness, turned within, begins to resume its normal state of calmness, peace, and joy. This is similar to deep states of meditation—the difference being that deep sleep is passive—it happens *to* us rather than through our actively taking part. Deep meditation or true superconsciousness is actively achieved and takes a great deal more energy to enter than the passive, deep sleep state of semi-superconsciousness. Superconsciousness is infinitely more desirable and rewarding than semi-superconsciousness. It is important to understand that, enticing though the thought may be, it is impossible for us to *sleep* our way into Self-realization and oneness with God.

The conscious state is marked by restlessness; the subconscious state, by a mixture of restfulness and activity, while bliss reigns in the semi-superconscious and superconscious states. The ego is peaceful in the realm of semi-superconsciousness, subtly excited or pleased in the dream state, and grossly excited or pleased while experiencing the gross sensations of the conscious, wakeful state.

During waking hours the conscious state is predominant, with the subconscious and superconscious states trailing behind. By the power of concentration, we can make the subconscious or superconscious predominant. The conscious state of restlessness can be changed into the dreamy state of subconsciousness or the supremely peaceful state of superconsciousness. The wise person learns to change his or her center from conscious to superconscious predominance. In the next chapter, Yogananda's technique for willfully changing your level of consciousness at any time will be fully explained.

The average person generally concentrates and remains on the plane of physical consciousness. But when he is forcibly (through drugs) or passively (through fatigue) led to the subconscious chamber of dreams and quiet sleep, or when he enters the semi-superconsciousness of joyous, deep sleep, his ego seems to be only dimly conscious. The ordinary ego can support only one state at a time: the conscious, subconscious, or semi-superconscious. In the untrained ego, sidetracked on the path of upward evolution, the conscious state predominates. It loves to stay in, and be conscious of, the realm of the senses. It forgets that every night it moves semiconsciously through the chamber of dreams or through the deep, semi-superconscious sleep state toward Spirit.

But the ego *can* be trained, through meditation, to dwell more and more in the higher, permanently blissful state of superconsciousness—learning to release the impositions of the desire-controlled and sensory-manipulated conscious and subconscious minds.

Basic Levels of Consciousness

1. **The Conscious State**—generally predominates, with subconsciousness and superconsciousness trailing behind, because we concentrate and try to stay on a plane of physical consciousness; a waking state; attachment to operating through the five senses; the ego stays awake and excited by gross sensations and sensory input; the average person is said

to think approximately twelve thousand thoughts a day! Two things generally lead us from consciousness to subconsciousness: (a) fatigue, by which we are passively led to subconsciousness, and (b) drugs or such things, by which we are forcibly plunged into subconsciousness.

2. **The Subconscious State**—the abode of memories, habits, and dreams; a lower state of energy than the regular conscious state; a time of a mixture of activity and restfulness; a time of dreaming, light sleep, or even daydreaming, woolgathering, "spacing out"; in a subconscious state the ego is still subtly excited, but not as much as in the conscious state. Ordinary dreams come from the subconscious state.

3. **The Semi-Superconscious State**—deep, joyous sleep; unalloyed enjoyment of impermanent peace in which we *temporarily* regain our normal and true state of calmness, peace, and joy. This state is passive or negative in the sense that we are not able to sustain it indefinitely. We "fall" into this deep-sleep state rather than entering it through will power and self-effort, showing the important difference between semi-superconsciousness and superconsciousness.

4. **The Superconscious State**—positive peace, calmness, and joy, attained actively, not passively. We do not "fall" passively into superconsciousness. Rather, with God's help, we uplift our consciousness, attaining superconsciousness with energy, determination, and will power. Superconsciousness is the complete cessation of unrest, the soul's awareness of unending expansion, unhampered by friction-producing sensations. The ego is finally at peace, having identified itself completely with the soul or the divine presence within.

CHAPTER SEVEN

Ordinary Dreams vs. Superconscious Visions

I will abhor nightmares of ignorant acts. I will love dreams of noble achievements. I will love all dreams of goodness, for they are Thy dreams. I may dream many dreams, but I am ever awake, thinking of Thee.

—from the *Praecepta Lessons* (1938) by Paramhansa Yogananda

Dreams Should Not Be Imposed upon Us

Paramhansa Yogananda often emphasized that we should gain such control over our consciousness that ordinary dreams are no longer imposed on us. We must learn to dream (or have superconscious visions) at will. We should not allow intruding thoughts, memories, habits, sensations, and vagrant thoughts to pull our attention away from what it is we want to dream.

When we are able to free our attention from all distractions—then we can focus it on the things we want to dream about. The desired dream will follow, if no other thoughts are allowed to intrude upon our attention. Yogananda suggests that we remember these important points concerning the difference between ordinary dreaming and superconscious visions:

1. Superconscious visions are true and can help us spiritually.

2. Subconscious, ordinary, or meaningless dreams are to be avoided, for these types of dreams generally offer neither pure rest nor beneficial instruction.

3. Don't wish to dream in the ordinary way, but seek rather to have true visions of divine realities in the light of God's presence within.

Here we see how Yogananda makes a strong distinction between superconscious visions and ordinary subconsciously produced dreams. He further explains that visions can happen while awake or asleep, and with eyes open or closed. This kind of vision has an entirely different feeling or quality than a dream has. A vision produces a much greater feeling of heightened awareness, blessing, and joy—very different from what we experience in our regular dream states.

Divine Visions

Divine visions are created during the wakeful state by the all-seeing, all-powerful superconsciousness. At certain times the superconsciousness uses brain energy to materialize thoughts about a true event which will happen in the near or far future, and displays them during the wakeful state with the eyes open or closed.

When a true vision is seen with open eyes, the life-force is projected from the brain into the ether. In this case the people and scenes viewed may not be "true-to-touch," but they are "true-to-vision." Furthermore, what is shown will evolve to be true in every sense in the future, if one's spiritual development continues.

Nightmares come under the category of "subconsciously induced dreams." During a nightmare, more energy is used by one's heart and circulation, and the breath becomes more excited.

Superconsciously induced dreams have a much more peaceful effect on your body. The breath, heartbeat, and entire physical and vital processes relax. When we have a superconscious dream, our breathing patterns and heartbeat are slower than when we have nightmares or ordinary subconscious dreams.

As has been said before, sleep is subconscious sensory and muscular relaxation, which happens as our life-force passively retires into the spine and brain. So, in an ordinary dream, our relaxed energy passes through "grooves" in the subconscious part of the brain, where subconscious experiences (memories) are stored. When this happens we have an ordinary or subconscious dream.

How Superconscious Visions Take Place

True superconscious visions, however, are produced when we are able to consciously withdraw the energy from the muscles and the heart region and direct it to the point between the eyebrows (the frontal lobe, which constitute the more spiritually developed part of the brain, as opposed to the medulla oblongata, which is more closely related to the subconscious mind). As soon as this kind of vision comes, the breath and heart become much slower or may cease altogether.

For superconscious visions to take place, the soul uses the power of intuition and inner sight to "photograph" certain events from the cosmos. Superconscious dreams are also projected on the screen of intuition, as opposed to ordinary dreams, which are projected on the screen of the subconscious mind. The soul uses subjective intuition to photograph certain superconscious experiences or events; then it adds this subjective intuition to the relaxed energy from the body and finally materializes visions on the screen of objective intuition, producing the motion pictures of superconscious vision.

Superconsciously induced dreams (as opposed to superconscious visions), when experienced by the subconscious mind, are dreams in which the soul takes a real intuitive experience and with that intuition, projects itself into a dream. In superconscious dreams, the soul, as the operator, projects pictures on the screen of intuition. Because the soul does not take any film from the subconscious, it photographs events from the cosmos using the lens of intuition, and projects them as superconscious dreams.

Semi-superconscious dreams are not consciously induced but have a touch of superconsciousness in them. Sometimes while dozing, one beholds a little vision produced by a combination of the subconscious, superconscious, and conscious minds. Consciously produced superconscious dreams are a mixture of the subconscious, semi-superconscious, and conscious minds. A mingling of those three states can produce a semi-superconscious vision.

Superconscious dreams occur when the superconscious mind drops a true experience directly into the subconscious mind and thus produces a different sort of dream (superconscious!). On these occasions, the ego plays no conscious part.

There is another, even spiritually higher kind of "super-vision," in which one can see and touch and talk to a saint or master—it is possible for a spiritual seeker to successfully invite a saint to materialize himself. This type of vision is created when Christ consciousness suffuses the superconsciousness and employs a combination of cosmic energy and divine will to materialize invisible saints and masters into the conscious minds of spiritually developed disciples.

Sometimes in superconscious dreams, the superconsciousness (which dwells in all time frames—past, present, and future—simultaneously) photographs a real future happening and drops it into the dream-movie-house to be filmed and projected there for the guidance of the ego. These dreams, good or bad, always come true. The superconsciousness is especially interested in offering messages which will awaken and motivate the seeker to turn away from sense pleasures and return to his home of permanent bliss in God. Besides occasionally offering true superconscious dreams, the superconsciousness can also insert into regular subconscious dreams hints of spiritual progress and God's call to the soul.

Remember that by our superconscious will, we can create any dream. Visions are real, while subconscious dreams are only imaginary images. Visions of true future happenings, produced by superconsciousness, are very useful, for they can guide and mold our lives. A spiritually developed person seldom dreams false, ordinary, or useless subconscious dreams. The ability to dream at will signifies that your will can materialize thoughts, and that you are on the cusp of receiving true guiding visions. Superconscious visions are best evoked by going deep into meditation and wishing to see the real state of things. But before you can draw to yourself a true superconscious vision, you must be able to dream at will. Techniques for controlling your dreams or "dreaming at will" are discussed in the following chapter.

Please remember that a superconscious vision would never be the same thing as a deluded or imaginary hallucination created from one's egoic desire. They are given to us as gifts from God and as a result of many years of deep meditation.

Somnambulism and Hypnosis

Before closing this chapter, it might be helpful to comment about two related subjects: hypnosis and somnambulism.

Somnambulism (sleepwalking or other nocturnal body movements) occurs when the ego uses certain subconscious films not only to produce a picture, but also to move the muscles and limbs as a way of acting out a dream-movie. The subconscious temporarily controls what is normally a conscious process. While awake and walking, or otherwise moving in some way, we are aware of what we are consciously willing our bodies to do. In somnambulism, walking or other body movements are directed by the subconscious, not the conscious mind. Certain subconscious experiences can take hold of the conscious processes, and then the body works out that subconscious impulse in movement.

Somnambulism can be dangerous and is certainly not conducive to restful sleep. It is generally a product of too much stress and restlessness in the wakeful state.

Although there are situations in which hypnotism may be justified, such as when it is used as a substitute for anesthesia when anesthesia may pose a danger, yogis generally warn against repeated hypnosis sessions.

Hypnosis takes place when someone other than ourselves arouses our subconscious mind in order to control our conscious mind. It happens when, by certain suggestions or techniques, someone stimulates our subconsciousness and tells it to take control of our consciousness, giving it directions and suggestions. Repeated sessions of deep hypnosis could take away our mental freedom, for it allows an outside force to use the subconscious to overpower the conscious mind, a process that could endanger our brains and weaken our will power.

Meditation vs. Hypnosis

In his book *Meditation for Starters*, Swami Kriyananda addresses the question: "In what way is meditation different from hypnosis or self-hypnosis?"

Answer: "Hypnosis opens the mind *downward*; it increases our susceptibility to subconscious influences. Both hypnosis and self-hypnosis can be helpful for working on those influences and changing them if they are harmful. Neither form of hypnosis, however, improves discrimination, which descends from a level of superconscious awareness.

"What hypnosis does is blur the threshold between conscious and subconscious awareness. It makes the conscious mind, in turn, more susceptible to subconscious influences in general. The long-range effect of both hypnosis and self-hypnosis, therefore, is to weaken the will power. This effect is particularly insidious if one allows oneself to be repeatedly hypnotized by other persons.

"Consciously directed affirmations to the subconscious, on the other hand, produce positive results, particularly when they are then offered upward to the superconscious. For self-transformation occurs, finally, when the resolution to change is charged with superconscious awareness, and thence fully absorbed into the subconscious."

Chapter Eight

Taking Charge of Our Dreams

O God, if we must dream,

Teach us to dream beautiful dreams.

—from the poem "If We Must Dream" by Paramhansa Yogananda, *Inner Culture* magazine, August 1937

Swami Kriyananda talks of his experience in directing the plot of his dreams: "When I was in college, I wanted to become a playwright. This calling was very strong in me for a few years and even influenced my dreams. Often while I was dreaming some situation happened or some character came into the dream and I went along with it for a while. But then my 'playwright persona' reasserted itself and I thought, 'Well, this person or situation is not helping the plot. Let's go back and change it.' So I would go back and take the person out of the dream or change the situation to my liking. Then I was satisfied with the dream. I felt it to be a good plot now."

He continues on this subject: "We dream it all. We make up our own plot and everything. It's really amazing how many different worlds we live in, even though everybody seems to be going through the same basic dramas. Still, there are as many life stories and nuances to those stories as there are human beings."

In order to take more control of our waking lives, Paramhansa Yogananda suggests that we begin controlling our dreams. He says that we should "become the king of the three kingdoms of the mind: subconscious, conscious, and superconscious, and be able to enter and exit those states of consciousness *at will!*"

Meditation is the primary method of entering the superconscious realms. But also, by learning to control our eye positions and shifting the gaze at will (see the technique outlined below), we can gradually transfer our egos from the conscious world of sense perceptions to the tranquility of the subconscious dream world, or to the superconscious state of perfect joy.

Yogananda says: "Think of the freedom you can gain by learning to shift, at will, from the land of terrestrial horror to the land of beautiful dreams. And then, when even the dream fairies bother you, you are able to float in the ether of eternal serenity or superconscious bliss where dreams dare not tread or disturb your perfect peace. Then you truly become the king of three kingdoms. *Realize this!* Do not remain imprisoned in, and identified with, the little island-prison of the body!"

He continues: "The yogi can do just as he pleases. He can live in the realm of the senses, or fly to the land of dreams, or float in the vast ocean of eternal bliss. He may choose superconscious serenity or subconscious dreams; or he may give predominance to semi-superconsciousness or superconsciousness. If the yogi prefers, it is possible to remain half conscious and half dreaming, or half conscious and half asleep yet dreamless, or semi-superconscious and half dreaming, or quietly subconscious. If none of these pleases the yogi, he or she may elect to enjoy conscious sensations, dream tranquility, subconsciousness, semi-superconsciousness, and superconsciousness all at the same time. When such an incredible level of control is possible, then the throne of consciousness, instead of resting on a little speck of sensation, or a 'diamond-chip' of dream, or a little shining ambition, becomes fixed in the sparkling bosom of Omnipresence."*

Yogananda's Technique for Changing Your Level of Consciousness at Will

Relax your body in a sitting position. Sit comfortably, leaning against the back of your chair. Close your eyes and let them droop downward. Forget your worries, dismissing all restless thoughts; feel drowsy, become passive and mentally careless; in other words, let go, fall asleep, or at least try to doze. Repeat this several times until the moment you lower the searchlight of your vision (the eyes) by closing them and switching off the optical currents, you are instantly submerged in the subconscious dreamland of sleep.

Then, when you are heavy with sleep, quickly tense the whole body, sit upright with a straight spine, and open wide and lift your eyes so that they are in a level position, looking forward in front of you. Keep looking at one object without winking. Take a deep, invigorating breath and banish sleep at will!

Now once again close your eyes, letting them droop downward, relax the whole body, and instantly fall into sleep again.

Every night, before dropping off to sleep, command your subconscious mind to wake you at a different hour. Continue making this suggestion to the subconscious until it obeys. Fall asleep with the thought that a matter of vital importance depends upon your getting up at your appointed hour.

After you have trained your subconscious mind to fall asleep instantly or to waken you at will, practice fixing your vision at the point between the eyebrows, and instantaneously go consciously into the state of profound peace and intoxicating joy. The regular practice of deep meditation will help you develop this ability.

Calm your mind and release all thoughts. Every time thoughts

---

* *Super-Advanced Course No. 1* (1930) by Paramhansa Yogananda, Lesson 3, "Reversing the Searchlights of the Senses."

return, firmly dismiss them. Then meditate on peace; be drunk with it; merge into it.

Remember, to gain dominion over the three kingdoms of your consciousness, you must practice these exercises as often as possible. Whenever you have a few minutes of leisure, lower your closed eyes and enter the "kingdom of dreams" at will. Then awaken at will by opening and leveling your eyes and, entering the "kingdom of wakeful consciousness," drink in the beauties of nature all around you. Then lift your vision to the point between the eyebrows and enter the superconscious "kingdom of bliss."

You can attain complete freedom from worldly cares only after you have learned to shift the searchlight of your eyes, your attention, and your energy from the conscious to the subconscious plane or from the conscious to the superconscious plane, either dreaming or enjoying superconscious bliss at will. Then you can fly from the plane of sensations to the plane of dreams or to the realm of eternal peace, as you choose. Remember, however, that as you shift your vision from the conscious to the subconscious, the life force and energy must also be switched off from the lamps of the billion-celled muscles, and the visual, auditory, olfactory, tactual, and gustatory nerves. In shifting from the conscious to the superconscious plane, your lungs must be breathless, your heart calm, your cells inactive, your circulation stilled, as you listen to the symphony of the cosmic vibration of AUM. This advanced spiritual state is known to yogis as an early stage of "samadhi" (oneness with Spirit).

In a brief but very interesting video clip of Yogananda (the source is an old newsreel made when he was visiting England in 1936), he demonstrates his ability to shift his consciousness instantly from subconscious, to conscious, to superconscious states. This video was released by Crystal Clarity Publishers under the title, "Yogananda in Samadhi," and is definitely worth watching. In it you will be able to see what changing eye positions and levels of consciousness actually look like. Here is a transcription of what he says during this video, which might also be titled "How to Sleep Correctly":

"Yoga is not magic, sword-swallowing, or crystal gazing. But it is the art of super-living as discovered by the ancient sages of India in 1500 B.C.

"If the Western brothers only could learn the methods of the yogis, then they would learn to live a hundred years in perfect health, happiness, and great success.

"You people do not sleep correctly and allow your sleep to be disturbed by the mental movie of dreams. You subconsciously worry about unpaid bills and troubles.

[He lies down on a couch.]

"The reason for lying in this posture is to keep the internal organs floating in the tray of the chest and abdomen, free from any pressure. But by closing the eyes [he closes his eyes] and inner relaxation, I can remain asleep several nights.

"And by opening the eyes and recharging the body [he does this], I can keep awake several days.

"Now, I will go into the state of superconscious bliss, by lifting my eyes [his open eyes turn upward instantly and remain unblinking], higher relaxation, and [by] controlling my heartbeat."

The Art of Dreaming at Will and Controlling the Contents of Your Dreams as Taught by Paramhansa Yogananda

To will dreams and visions: Superconscious visions can be had only by going deep into a superconscious state of meditation and then wishing to see the real state of things. But before one can have a true superconscious vision, it helps to be able to dream at will (to consciously direct your dreams).

The art of dreaming at will: Sit in your dimly lighted bedroom just before you feel sleepy. With half-open eyes steadily and simultaneously look at a portion of the room, trying to visualize and memorize every detail. While doing this, will yourself to see all the objects you are currently seeing later in a dream. Now fall asleep while you are visualizing/memorizing what you are seeing. In this way you will be able to visualize or produce a mechanical vision of anything, any person, or any place in a dream consciously produced in the subconsciousness.

Ordinarily, dreams are not given to you from an outside source. They are created by your conscious, subconscious, or superconscious mind. Hence, by your conscious or subconscious mind during sleep, or by superconscious will, and with practice, you can create any dream you wish.

Remember that superconscious visions are real, while dreams are only subconscious images. Being able to produce superconscious visions of true future happenings is a very powerful and useful ability, for in developing this ability you can begin to mold your life into a model of spiritual perfection.

A spiritually developed person seldom experiences false dreams. To dream at will signifies that, using your will power, you can materialize thoughts, and that soon you will be able to produce truth-guided superconscious visions.

With enough practice in focusing your will power to change your level of consciousness at will and to dream specific dreams at will, you will someday be able to become conscious during the dream state—Yogananda calls this becoming "semi-super-conscious." This state is difficult to describe, but it is possible to attain and has been achieved by many. Some dream-workers call this process "Lucid Dreaming." Lucid dreaming is knowing we are dreaming, while in the dream state. After that awareness comes, some people can direct or control their dreams. There are a number of books available on this subject which describe various techniques to help you direct the course of your dreams. Specific examples of "semi-superconscious dreams" are offered later in this chapter.

Does Yogananda recommend that we work nightly to achieve a state of "Lucid Dreaming"? Aside from the techniques mentioned above, he does not delve further into this subject. But it seems evident from an overview of his teachings that it would be wise for the truth seeker to practice manifesting *at will* all the different levels of consciousness available.

We should waste as little time and energy as possible in subconscious sleep and ordinary dreaming. In fact, most of the great spiritual masters are reported as needing little or no sleep. Yogananda often said that he rarely slept at all! He frequently demonstrated to his disciples that even when he seemed to be asleep, he was fully aware of all that was going on around him. He said that occasionally he would let his mind go into subconsciousness in order to empathize with the people around him who were forced nightly to enter the subconscious state of sleep. He added, wryly, that it was *not* pleasant for him to be subconscious, because he was used to being in a constant state of superconsciousness.

However, if in the process of learning to take control over our levels of consciousness, we work toward trying to have superconscious visions rather than ordinary dreams, we can infer that the intermediate step of becoming aware while dreaming and then taking charge of the course of our dreams, could be an important step toward full control of these different states of consciousness. In any case, it is vital to recognize the difference between subconscious sleep/ordinary dreaming and semi-superconscious dreams or superconscious visions. The lower states of consciousness inevitably drop away as the higher states move in to take their place. Eventually, all these states of consciousness merge into cosmic consciousness.

The Semi-Superconscious Dreams of Kamala Silva

According to Yogananda, semi-superconscious dreams can take place while we are seemingly still asleep. In these sorts of dreams, the soul "awakes" or become conscious, and a combination of true intuition and the subconscious "dream-maker" produces a true dream (prophetic, enlightening, or otherwise spiritually helpful).

Kamala Silva became a disciple of Yogananda at the age of fifteen. As his lifelong follower she continued to make great spiritual advances throughout her life. In 1964 she published an autobiographical work, *The Flawless Mirror*, describing her experiences with her guru, Paramhansa Yogananda. In this fascinating book (available through Crystal Clarity Publishers), she describes many spiritual visions, which she experienced on a fairly regular basis, but most particularly after Yogananda left his body in 1952. I highly recommend this book!

(Kamala often refers to her guru as "Master," as do most of Yogananda's disciples. This title does not indicate a slave/master relationship; rather, it honors the guru as one who has attained perfect *self*-mastery, and who has the power and intention to help his followers do the same.)

What follows is a description of one of her semi-superconscious experiences, taken from *The Flawless Mirror*, chapter 20, "My Guru Brings Dulcet Reminders of God." In this fascinating book, she offers many unusual descriptions of becoming conscious while sleeping, and of her semi-superconscious dreams. She calls them "Conscious Sleep States."

"I go to sleep naturally and then become aware, but without thought of the physical body which continues sleeping. I am conscious of what is happening as it occurs. It takes place in the *present* and I *participate*, thinkingly. I need not waken afterward (being already conscious) but simply open my eyes to see my immediate surroundings.

"In sleep the life energy (prana) is partially withdrawn into the spine and brain from the sensory and motor nerves, leaving the body completely relaxed. It is therefore an ideal time for spiritual receptivity, if one is consciously aware. . . ."

Holy Communion from Master

"I became conscious during sleep and was standing at the door of a large room where many disciples were present. I recognized many of them. Master [Paramhansa Yogananda] was presiding at this gathering. He was seated on a quite low platform. I entered the room and one of the Sisters led me up to him. His gaze rested upon me, and I saw he held a communion wafer. I knelt and my Guru placed the wafer in my mouth. I could feel it on my tongue. He then took my hand in both of his saying, 'This will tingle a little,'—and a *current* went from his hands into mine, and I could feel it travel up my arm and directly to my heart. By concentrating I could hold it there, or rather, keep aware of its gently permeating force. After the blessing imparted in these vibrations, and through the symbolic wafer, he asked me to repeat these words: *'Saints Always.'* This I did. Then I was again in my room and still suffused with the sacred blessing."

Requesting a Dream from God

To close this chapter, I would like to introduce a new slant on the subject of taking charge of our dreams. This idea came into focus recently when a friend spoke of a powerful dream she had had, and of how the dream had come to her and had helped her greatly.

At the time of this dream, Julie was the mother of three small children and has found it extremely challenging to find time to meditate. Because of this, she prayed that God would come to her in her dreams. Shortly after this prayer, she dreamed she was a prisoner in a Nazi concentration camp. "It was as horrible as anything you've heard or could imagine," she said. "I saw children taken from their mothers, and priests trying to pray but being dragged off. Still I could feel the divine courage within those subjected to these experiences. It was not the dark pit of despair I had imagined. I prayed to feel God in my dreams, and I literally could feel Him in the form of courage—something I personally needed. Also I could see how much all my fellow prisoners and I loved God. We prayed constantly and lived with nothing but God's presence—it was all we had in this world. It was awe-inspiring and blissful! Who could have imagined so much God-consciousness in the midst of such complete misery?

"Upon awakening I thought, strangely enough, that I might wish to return to the horrors of the concentration camp—simply because God was so perfectly present for me there. Also upon awakening I realized two things: 1) God had answered my prayer and had come to me through the gift of this inspiring dream; and, 2) if God could be so perfectly present with all of us in that prison, then certainly He can be with me in every moment of my hectic life."

What a great concept! Why not, like Julie, pray for a God-filled dream, a dream of inspiration and deep meaning, a dream with a message of hope, divine guidance, or a way of understanding our lives in new and better ways? Taking charge of our levels of consciousness, dreaming at will, directing the content of our dreams—all these are valuable talents to develop and exercises that Paramhansa Yogananda strongly suggests we practice. But occasionally, try asking God to produce and direct a special dream for you. You might be surprised and gratified at the results.

CHAPTER NINE

Using Dreams to Contact Departed Loved Ones

From this sleep, Lord, will you wake me?

From this dream, Lord, will you wake me?

In Thee I'm born, in Thee I die,

To live forever in Thee! . . .

O life is sweet,

And death a dream,

When Thy song flows through me.

—from the lyrics of two chants in *Cosmic Chants* (1938 edition) by Paramhansa
Yogananda

In *Letters to Truthseekers*, Swami Kriyananda wrote: "Love
forms a magnet, drawing souls together even after the separation
of death. Life as we know it is a dream; its characters come and go.
The scenes ever shift, often—so it would seem—without regard
for any consistent purpose."

He then added: "But just as the dreamer remains the same person through a succession of subconscious dreams, so also does the soul remain unchanged through a succession of life and death experiences. And even so does the thread of love continue through eternity, forever consistent, forming its own divine purpose. Divine love is indeed the only truly consistent fact in creation."

The Relationship Between Death and Dreams

"To those who grieve over the death of a loved one, the following words of [Yogananda's] should offer deep consolation.

"'Departed relatives and friends sometimes come to one in dreams. Be open to that possibility, especially if you deeply miss your loved ones, for such dreams can be true experiences.

"'When Woody's [a close woman disciple of Yogananda's] mother died of breast cancer, I became very withdrawn for a time. . . .

"'I prayed deeply. Then at last I saw her in the astral world.

"'An angel was leading her away from me. I saw her pause briefly and smile at the beauty of the flowers in a meadow. I called to her, and she turned. At first she didn't recognize me. But then I touched her on the forehead, and she cried, "I remember!" She parted the gown she was wearing and said, "See: no more cancer!" She was free, and wonderfully happy.'"*

Contacting the Souls of the Departed

Is it possible to use dreams as a way of contacting the souls of those who have departed this earth? Paramhansa Yogananda declares it to be so. But he first offers cautions. Then he explains how it can be done.

From Yogananda's early lessons:

Question: How can we get in touch with the dead?

Do not try to contact "tramp souls" who infest the ether with their presence. As tramps can occupy and run to destruction an empty, unlocked automobile, so tramp souls can get into absent-

---

* From *Conversations with Yogananda* by Swami Kriyananda.

minded, shallow-brained people who try to invoke spirits through a passive state of mind. Such tramp souls can possess the brain and wreck it. Only true souls who loved you, and who continue to love you, should be invited. You need good souls to help you, and you can also send them help. Commune only with the highest saints. The tramp souls who come to you uninvited only want a free ride on your "brain-car" in order to wreck it. That is why people who passively allow themselves to be possessed usually lose their character, mind, and spiritual power.

Question: How do we invite good souls to visit us?

Concentrate deeply with patience until you can see your spiritual eye (a silver-white, five pointed star within an opal-blue globe, encased in a golden aurora) with open or closed eyes. You must be able to hold it as long as you want. Then visualize the good soul you want to meet and constantly broadcast to him to come into the light of the spiritual eye. If you have patience and a strong personal zeal, you will see and speak to that image, as in a talking picture, on the screen of the spiritual eye.

By deeper development, you will be able to see that soul with open eyes—and if a soul like Jesus accepts your invitation, not only can he be visible to you when your eyes are open, but he can so vibrate his body grossly—and synchronize sound, light, and touch sensations—that you can also hear and touch him. Bad souls cannot enter the entrenched, highly electrified orb of the spiritual eye. They become "astra-electrocuted." Only good souls who can help you can make themselves visible in the spiritual eye.

Question: Can souls be contacted if they have left the astral plane and been reborn on earth?

Yes. When someone very near to you dies and you find it impossible to forget him or her, even though you have traveled far away through the arches of the years, it is still possible to find your loved one in the following way. After meditating deeply for an hour or more, lift your hand and concentrate on the fingertips.

Concentrate also at the point between the eyebrows (the spiritual eye), and continuously will yourself to contact the astral body of your departed loved one. Keep on turning your hand very gently in a circle toward north, south, east, west, northeast, southeast, and so on. At each direction in the circle around which your hand moves, try to feel the presence of the astral body of the departed. When your fingers feel that you have touched this person as you used to touch him or her while alive, your heart will be thrilled. Keep on visualizing the person in the spiritual eye and he or she will appear there. Then ask your fingers and heart to indicate in what place your friend is reborn, according to the direction you felt him through your fingers. When you feel this soul through your fingers and heart, you may see and talk to this loved one, and he or she will tell you if he or she is in the astral world. If the soul has since been reborn on earth, the location can be revealed. Then there will be great rejoicing.[*]

If one of your loved ones has already reincarnated, and you are still unable to contact him or her by the above process, you can signal to the ever-awake astral body and receive an answer later within a dream, in sleep, or in the form of a superconscious vision in meditation.

By finding friends in this life and following them up in the astral sphere after death, you will perceive the mystery of life after death. Then you will know that death separated your loved ones from you so that you might love not only them and exclude all your other human brothers and sisters, but that you might give your love to all people in all incarnations. Thus when your heart becomes big enough to love all, you will know the Father who loves all His children alike—and knowing Him, you will know all your many parents and friends that you loved before. With that intense love you will learn to love all your animate and inanimate

---

[*] Yogananda relates an amazing story of how he located a young student of his named Kashi, who had died and was reborn nearby in India. (See chapter 28 of the first (1946) edition of *Autobiography of a Yogi*, titled "Kashi, Reborn and Rediscovered.")

brothers as your brothers and as children of your one, ever-kind, ever-mysterious Father-Mother-God.

Note well: Do not think constantly about a departed soul unless you know that he is good, and unless you feel an undying desire to reach him. If time cannot make you forget a departed friend, then try to contact him. If, day and night, you miss a dear friend, then you will have a sort of longing, a soothing presence around your heart. This will indicate to you that this friendly soul is trying to get in touch with you through your feeling, but he or she cannot materialize himself/herself because of your constant mental restlessness. But if you concentrate upon the feeling that your friend is present, doing this for several minutes just before falling asleep, then that friend will appear to you in a dream.

CHAPTER TEN

Dream Interpretation and Symbols in Dreams

Is there,

hidden in the heart of night,

blazing in secrecy,

light, like a billion suns,

truth eternal,

love divine,

awaiting our ardent search,

beckoning us on to perfection?

Is there some clue awaiting us,

slender but shining,

a golden thread, wind-borne into the night,

curving its way far and far to an answer?

—from the poem "A Search for Meaning" by Swami Kriyananda, excerpted from his book *Yours—The Universe!*

Symbols in Our Lives and in Our Dreams

Symbolism plays an important part in our lives, whether or not we consciously recognize it. Not only in our dreams, but also in almost every waking moment, we are influenced by symbols all around us. This book cannot do justice to this fascinating topic, but if it is of special interest to you, I would recommend these chapters in Swami Kriyananda's excellent book *The Hindu Way of Awakening:* chapter 2: "What Are Symbols?"; chapter 3: "The Power of Symbolism"; and chapter 6: "Symbolism: Truth, or Imagination?"

In chapter 6 of that book, Swami Kriyananda offers these explanations regarding symbols in dreams:

"Paramhansa Yogananda once made a fascinating statement, which I'll paraphrase here: 'The sun and moon are symbols of the Father and Mother aspects of God: Wisdom from the sun, Love from the moon. . . .'

"Symbols are usually thought of as objective *projections* of subjective ideas. Overlooked is the fact that consciousness itself is not only subjective, but universal. How, indeed, could it not have existed already at least as a potential, for life ever to have manifested it?

". . . [A]lthough God seeks communion with us in our souls above all, He also seeks to guide and inspire us through natural phenomena. The rain, Paramhansa Yogananda said, is a message to us of Divine Compassion; the flowers whisper to us of God's love and joy; the tenderness of Mother Nature reminds us of the consciousness in which She wants us always to live. On the other hand, Her elemental fierceness is also a warning to us not to live proudly, as if we were above divine law. Symbolism is not only a projection of human imagination: It is inherent in all phenomena."

Carl Jung and Dream Symbols

"Carl Jung . . . claimed that certain symbols are universal, in the sense that they belong to what he called the 'collective unconscious' of mankind. His term 'unconscious' is not wholly felicitous, inasmuch as nothing, really, is wholly without consciousness. In human beings there are powerful urges, such as the instinct for self-preservation, over which people have no conscious control, but which are conscious enough themselves to seize control over the power of both will and reason.

"Jung would have done better . . . to speak of a 'subtle network of awareness.' For we are all part of one reality. What affects us in a deep way affects all, be it with our suffering or our joy. The enlightenment of one saint uplifts, to however slight a degree, the entire human race. This 'network' doesn't exist, however, on lower-than-conscious levels of awareness, but on higher than conscious. In subconsciousness we withdraw into ourselves, away from objective reality; subconsciousness, therefore, separates us from the rest of reality. It is in superconsciousness that our true unity with all life can be experienced.

"There are lower levels of consciousness than that which produces conscious thought. And there are also higher. The thoughts produced by human reason are like heavy trucks, shifting gears downward to lumber their way up every grade of rational difficulty. On higher levels of consciousness, however, the mind soars like a bird, high above the mountain peaks of all difficulties. In this greater-than-normal awareness, all that exists participates to some degree. In superconsciousness, even the apparently inanimate rocks play a role. Neither rocks nor most of humanity are aware of the latent superconscious within them, but that level of consciousness never ceases to be aware of them. It knows the slightest movement of every atom.

"The ancient teaching of India is that God dreamed the universe into existence. Everything is part of that cosmic dream, even as the waves are part of, and united by, the vast ocean beneath them.

Symbols Possessing Universal Relevance

"Within the fundamental unity of consciousness, certain symbols possess universal relevance. The ocean . . . is one such symbol. So also are the sun and the moon. Another one is the cross. . . . Other symbols with universal resonance include a tall, straight tree; a round dot or perfect circle; a triangle; a candle or any small flame; a ship sailing calmly on the broad sea; a dark tunnel at the end of which shines a bright light; a high and symmetrically shaped mountain; a freshly opened rosebud; a lotus lifting itself in purity above the muddy water; a rainbow; a flowing river; the crescent moon; a five-pointed star; a six-pointed star or 'star of David,' one triangle of which reaches upward in aspiration to receive divine grace, descending with the other triangle; a golden aureole; the horizon line of the sea. We may dream of these things superconsciously, regardless of our religious beliefs or social upbringing. Each of them contains eternal and not merely ephemeral meaning."

Subconscious Symbols vs. Superconscious Symbols

In his teachings, Paramhansa Yogananda explains that symbols in dreams are of two basic types: subconscious and superconscious. Eventually—through longer, deeper meditations and by leading a spiritually inclined life—we learn to recognize the difference between the two. When superconscious symbols (see the list below) begin to appear in our dreams more frequently and with a sense of deep calmness, it is a sign of spiritual progress and an indication that we are moving rapidly to superconscious union with God: a worthy goal!

Paramhansa Yogananda on Understanding the Contents of Our Dreams

All dreams have some significance, though not all dreams are true. Even "meaningless" dreams are reflections of a disordered, purposeless life. In fact, all dreams signify the state of one's consciousness: the worldly person has worldly dreams; the active person dreams of activity; the evil person has dreams of evil; imaginative people have fanciful dreams; and matter-of-fact people dream of daily occurrences. Someone filled with worry and fear has nightmares—which should warn him to change his attitude lest he attract the objects of his worry or fear, not only through his conscious thoughts, but also through the powerful vibrations of his subconscious thoughts. One who dwells too much on sexual matters dreams of sex, which signifies that he should make a conscious effort to dislodge from his mind those acquired conscious and subconscious sex impulses. Subconscious optimism brings forth comic dreams, but subconscious pessimism produces tragic dream films.

Subconscious "Comedy and Tragedy Dreams" and Their Symbols

Comedy dreams are entertainment given by the subconscious mind. Through this sort of dream, the subconscious requests the conscious mind to relax and to be less serious about life. Tragedy dreams are the subconscious hinting to the conscious mind that it should desist from formulating dramas of worries and fears.

Falling in dreams indicates that the dreamer should control sexual thoughts. Dreams of temptations hint that temptation is not a physical but a mental reality, and can be controlled by development of the will.

Beating or hurting others in dreams represents that the conscious mind should forego revengeful thoughts.

Seeing a lady in dreams signifies marriage.

Seeing a house, a mine, an office, furniture, palaces, shops, or money represents approaching prosperity, if some effort is made.

Sadness in a dream represents a looming sickness.

Flying in the light indicates spiritual development.

Flying in the dark indicates prosperity.

Waterfalls represent the end of bad karma.

Meaningless dreams are really nothing but "comedy dreams" and should be ignored.

Do not try to decipher the meaning of *every* dream. Put your energy into deciphering those that seem to have a superconscious message. Remember that until you are highly developed spiritually, most dreams will arise from your subconscious and symbolize your present mental or physical state; hence adjusting your conscious thoughts and daily actions in time will clarify and improve your dreams.

Superconscious Dream Hints and Symbols

In superconscious dreams, the superconsciousness photographs real future happenings and drops them into the dream-movie-house to be filmed there for the guidance of the ego. These dreams, good or bad, always come true. The superconsciousness is especially interested in releasing messages that will encourage the soul to return to its home of happiness in God. In addition to occasionally providing real dreams, the superconsciousness also gives dream hints of spiritual progress and of the call of God—hints that the dreamer had made spiritual strides in his past life, or in this life, and that it would be relatively easy for him to develop along those lines now, and that he would meet with little resistance.

Paramhansa Yogananda categorizes these "superconscious dream hints/symbols" more specifically, as follows:

"Whenever you dream *calmly* about huge fires, the ocean, or vast waters, rivers, boats, angels, scriptures, saints, temples, churches, altars, flowers, cloudless skies, sunny lights, auroras, or the moon, or of a feeling of expansion in space, then know that the time for your spiritual development is near to the working out of the effects of prenatal or postnatal bad actions (karma), by the power of right living in this life."

A huge fire represents the burning of past karma.

Light and the ocean signify vast perceptions of Self-realization in meditation.

Water represents the results of divine perceptions attainable by meditation.

A river suggests plying up the river of life force in the spine through yoga practices or meditation.

A boat indicates that one should seek the right guru; a divinely appointed teacher who is a human vehicle for messages from God; whose voice, intelligence, and spiritual perception the Divine uses to completely redeem the disciple in one or more incarnations. The guru is the "boat" or vehicle of salvation, or the "spiritual mariner" who takes the disciple across oceans of past karma to the shores of God-realization. A boat also represents Self-realization through the practice of the technique of salvation received from the guru.

Angels represent divine friends and saints in past lives who remember us and try to redeem us through silent suggestions of their presence.

Scriptures represent that the dreamer should follow the path of wisdom and study to attain his desired goal.

Saints represent the sages whom we specially adored in the past.

Temples indicate that one should follow the teachings of the Masters.

Churches indicate that one should worship God deeply according to the yogic method of real concentration, and not be absent-minded.

Altars represent communion with God, or marriage with an extremely divine soul. The real marriage and the happiest one lies in the divine union of the receptive feminine souls of all human beings, both male and female, with the only true masculine principle: God.

Cloudless skies represent a serene, pure path of communion with God—spiritual development without trouble, and an abundance of clear spiritual perceptions.

Flowers represent the budding of the blossoms of creative wisdom in the garden of thought. By the magic wand of "mere willingness," the spiritual seeker will find the right thought arising at the right time.

Sunny lights signify astral visions illumining vast spaces during meditation.

Auroras represent "cosmic astral light," in which one can see all the astral planets, large and small, glittering in space, and the visitation of cosmic consciousness during deepest meditation.

The moon indicates that one should combine devotion with astral visions perceived in meditation in order to progress on the spiritual path.

A feeling of expansion in space represents the experience of omnipresence during meditation.

Swami Kriyananda on Dream Analysis

In May 2006, I had an opportunity to ask Swami Kriyananda the following question:

Savitri: Is it worthwhile to try to analyze our dreams?

Swami Kriyananda: The difficulty with psychoanalysis, as we know it today, is that it makes people too self-conscious, just when what we need is to get away from being overly self-consciousness and self-involved. If we think: "I did this" and "I did that" and "I did the other thing," we are going to be pulled down by all these "I-thoughts."

We have a marvelous laboratory for testing this theory right here at Ananda Village. For nearly forty years, we've seen people come and go; and we've seen that in every case, those who were happiest were those who thought least about themselves, and those who never really found happiness were those who were always worrying about themselves and whether they were wrong about this or that in their past.

We need to get rid of that attitude—and the same applies to dream analysis. Too much dream analysis makes us preoccupied with ourselves.

Most dreams do not have the kind of significance that some people, who teach this kind of therapy, try to insist. Most dreams have no meaning at all, and are a product of subconscious ramblings.

In my book *Hope for a Better World,* I give a good example of this sort of overly analytical thinking.

After my "Glenn Miller dream" [described below] I woke up feeling, "Oh, that was good fun!" But if I had tried to analyze it in detail, I would have gotten nowhere. I think the most important thing about a dream is how you feel about it after you wake up. It's condensed into a feeling—do you feel good or do you feel bad?

There's *much* too much attention given to dream analysis.

However, sometimes a dream *is* a true superconscious dream. That kind of dream uplifts you, and that kind of dream one should be grateful for. It's wonderful to have such dreams! You see Paramhansa Yogananda and you feel bliss; or you see some other saint and you feel great joy—that's a blessing; hold to that!

Remember that we do get some karma from dreams, because there's still the thought: "*I* am doing this." So, if we wish to grow spiritually, we need to work on eliminating that thought.

Superconsciousness is the goal. Rather than spending much time analyzing subconscious dreams, it would better just to merge into that higher state.

From *Hope for a Better World* by Swami Kriyananda (J. Donald Walters)

"[Sigmund] Freud analyzed dreams . . . , claiming that in dreams people reveal their unfulfilled or repressed desires.

"Needless to say, valid insights into all this data require considerable sensitivity on the part of the psychoanalyst. Intellectual analysis is inadequate for this task, for deep perception requires also sympathy: Indeed, it requires intuition. Unfortunately, the word *analysis* suggests only an intellectual function. Given the direction of modern thought, no other method of diagnosis would be acceptably scientific.

"Deep feelings, however, cannot be understood by analysis alone any more than a song can be understood by impersonally observing the singer's gestures and expressions. Sympathy, especially *calm* sympathy, is essential for understanding people, much more so than detached analysis of them. Many men and women no doubt enter the psychiatric profession out of a desire to help others. Nevertheless, the training they receive conditions them to analyze people intellectually. For in the classroom they must learn the need for preserving scientific objectivity. The process is likely to deaden their natural empathy.

"I had an amusing dream recently. It was just before waking in the morning. I was to play a trombone solo with Glenn Miller's band. I've never played the trombone, and had never done so in the dream, either. I tried a few tentative notes, and was surprised that they came out mildly well. The band members smiled in appreciation for my effort; one of them called out, 'All *right!*' Their reaction was friendly and supportive, through hardly overwhelmed. Before I could continue, it seemed I was to sing a well-known Glenn

Miller number, 'Chattanooga Choo-Choo,' with Glenn Miller himself singing the introduction. This all took place in a studio, not on stage before a crowd. Song sheets were spread out before us on a piano top, and the pianist was about to begin playing when I awoke.

"Now then, what did this dream mean? Glenn Miller's was probably the best-known band in the early 1940s. He played the trombone superbly. A tie-in comes to mind: Two days earlier, I had noticed on a brochure for a new medical device the name, 'At Last.' This was also the name of a song Glenn Miller recorded many years ago for a movie. A tenuous link? Well, anyway, there you have it.

"Looking at my dream from a Freudian perspective, I can imagine a psychoanalyst saying that it portrayed wish fulfillment—or, if not that, then a fear of public embarrassment. Would either analysis be correct? There was no public in the dream, so of that particular fear we may say it wasn't likely; in fact, I wasn't fearful at all. The band members were friendly to me, and not in some way opposed to making it all happen. Was I in any other way emotionally engaged: nervous? apprehensive? competitive? overconfident? eager to show off? happy to find myself in the company of a famous person and with a prominent band? worried about the public's reception? pleased with the music? displeased with anything? concerned about my ability to perform well? None of the above. I was interested, but otherwise not involved. As far as I can tell, the dream had no meaning. When I awoke, it was with amusement over this quite trivial fantasy.

"A psychoanalyst, however, might see promising possibilities here. I've said the dream contained no wish fulfillment. 'Are you *sure?*' he might ask skeptically. 'Are you being completely honest with yourself?' I've said I felt no apprehension. 'You may only be fooling yourself' might be his warning. I've said I wasn't concerned about the public's reception, but (he might remind me) fear of appearing in public, and especially of speaking or performing on a stage, is one of mankind's major phobias. So then—who's to say?

"I imagine that any number of 'revelations' might be ferreted out of that dream, were a person so inclined. Yet when I awoke it was with a smile of amusement. I'd have dismissed it all from my mind if it hadn't occurred to me that this might make an interesting addition to the present chapter. A psychoanalyst, relying only on his intellect, might have much to say on the subject, but if he took my own feelings into account—and this *was my* dream, after all!—I think he'd soon close his notebook and look elsewhere for clues to the *real* Don Walters.

"As I contemplate dreams that I've found meaningful in my life—this wasn't one of them!—it seems to me that usually their message was not revealed so much in their literal content as in the feeling that lingered with me afterward. Sometimes this feeling conveyed a clear message. Sometimes the message itself hadn't much bearing on the events of the dream. What mattered was that I awoke with some new and deeper insight, or some new resolution. Feelings like these are subjective and personal; I wouldn't want others picking them apart. What the [meaningful] dreams accomplished was significant for their results, not for any analysis I might have made of their contents."

More on Dream Analysis

(The following is transcribed from a class given by the author at Ananda Village on Yogananda's teachings about dreams and dreaming.)

Question: "Should I try to dream at night and then remember and analyze my dreams?"

Savitri: "I don't know that I would attempt to *try* to dream. I don't know that I would attempt to try even to *remember* all my dreams. I realize that this flies in the face of most schools of thought around the subject of dreaming—in which they teach that it is a good idea to keep a dream journal and write down your dreams every night and analyze them in detail.

"I think that for those who sincerely follow a path of yoga and meditation, and from everything I've been able to locate in Yogananda's or Swami Kriyananda's teachings on this subject, it is clear that we need to focus our energy on the superconscious state attained primarily through deep meditation, rather than focusing on subconscious states like sleeping and dreaming. Dreaming is primarily a subconscious activity. True, we can have some important and instructive dreams. And it is true that the saints and masters can use dreams to contact us. Spirit can use a dream to help us or to give us encouragement or needed information. But most of our regular nightly dreams are *not* where our focus needs to be. Personally I have never bothered with keeping a dream journal, nor would I recommend that anyone do so."

Question: "But what if I have a dream that feels very important; it seems like it's trying to tell me something important and I don't understand what it is—should I just forget it?"

Savitri: "Not always. One way to approach this would be to use your meditations and your intuitive perceptions gained through meditation to find out what some of the elements of a seemingly important dream might mean.

"For example, I had a dream a few years ago in which I was hiking up a hill near where I live. I was close to the top when I had a strong feeling I should turn around and look behind me. There I saw two large wolves with big yellow eyes sitting calmly. They were just looking at me intently. I looked back at them, and I felt intensely that they were trying to tell me something. Then I realized that I probably ought to be afraid, because I was out there alone—they were very big, after all, and wolves are supposed to be dangerous! But somehow I realized that they weren't a danger to me, and further, that they wanted to communicate something of importance to me. That was all I remembered of the dream.

Because it was vivid and calm, I decided to try to find out if the dream had a special meaning or spiritual message for me.

"I remembered hearing that one of the greatest psychics of the last century, Edgar Cayce, was of the opinion that nothing of real importance happens to us in waking life without it first having been foreshadowed in our dreams. He stressed also that dreams are highly individual and that *we alone* are our own best dream interpreters. For me, the 'wolves' in my dream seemed to have a sort of 'foreshadowing' symbolism. Through meditation and a certain technique mentioned below, I was able to receive a strong impression of what was being foreshadowed in this dream—and so it proved to be. The dream actually did presage something that happened later in my life."

A Dream Analysis Technique

Here is the technique I used to understand my "two wolves dream." I have used this process successfully several times with dreams which, even though they may have been subconscious rather than superconscious, still seemed worthwhile to divine their meaning.

Although it is not taken directly from any yogic teachings I know of, it is based on Yogananda's recommendation that we use our meditations to develop intuitive guidance and inner understanding.

The technique: After you wake from what feels like an important or meaningful dream, immediately or as soon as possible, sit down and meditate. At the beginning of your meditation, in your mind review the dream briefly and pick out what seem to be two or three of the most important elements or symbols in the dream. These components probably represent some part of yourself. (For the dream I mentioned above, obviously it would have been those two large wolves.) Prayerfully ask the dream symbols: "Who are you? What part of me are you? What do you want to tell me?"

Then set these questions aside *completely* and continue with your usual meditation practices. At the end of the meditation, bring those questions back into your conscious mind and say, "OK, do you have anything to reveal to me *now?*" Quite possibly you will be in a more superconscious state—a state of consciousness that will allow the meaning of the symbols in your dream to become clearer to you. This may not happen right way; a clearer understanding may come to you later in the day or week. In any case, your intuition has been given the opportunity to tap into superconsciousness, where all true answers lie. If your dream symbols are meaningful or spiritually useful, they will be revealed to you; and you can learn something new about yourself or receive important guidance from your Higher Self.

The key elements in this technique are meditation, nonattachment, intuition,* and prayer. Pray for help in understanding the dream's symbols. If it is God's will that you know and if you can be benefited spiritually by this knowledge, then certainly it will come to you. Use the peaceful time at the close of your meditation to let the meaning of your dream become clear to you. Most of all, whether or not you receive a true understanding of the dream, leave it in God's hands.

Try using the following suggestions and template to guide you through the dream analysis process:

Analyzing Your Dreams

1. The first and most important suggestion: Don't ask someone else to analyze your dream. It's *your* dream and you alone are the best person to decipher its meaning(s).

2. Decide whether it is an important enough dream, sent to you by God or your own superconscious self. Otherwise, it would probably be best not to bother analyzing it. Most nightly dreams are based simply on threads of memories and subconscious

---

* For more specific information on using meditation to develop the power of intuition, I recommend the excellent book *Intuition for Starters* by J. Donald Walters (Swami Kriyananda).

meanderings and are meant more for entertainment than instruction.

3. Pray deeply for help and guidance. The best time to analyze a dream is at the close of your meditation.

4. Remember your dream as best you can (naturally the more quickly you can write down a few thoughts about your dream, just after you wake up, the more details you'll remember from the dream when you want to analyze it later).

5. Isolate three or four elements from the dream that seem to stand out, or have special importance to you, and list them (see below).

6. Then ask yourself this important question. *"What part of myself does this thing, person, situation (or whatever) represent?"*

Dream Analysis Worksheet

Stand-out items from your dream   **What part of me does this represent?**

1)

2)

3)

4)

Finally, humbly ask for divine guidance, that it may reveal to you any further message from the dream, especially as it may relate to your spiritual life and growth.

Review of Terminology

Conscious mind—works with the senses during wakeful hours, but sleeps (is unaware) at night.

Hallucinations—subconscious mental pictures, seen while awake, with open or closed eyes, but having no reality or meaning; often, but not always, drug-induced.

Hypnosis—someone arouses your subconscious mind and makes it control the conscious mind. Yogananda warns that hypnosis is not advisable because it weakens one's will power and takes away mental freedom.

Semi-superconscious dreams—happen while sleeping; the soul "awakes," and the combination of true intuition and the subconscious dream-maker produce a true dream (prophetic, enlightening, spiritually helpful); an answer to the desire to see the real state of things.

Somnambulism—hallucinations triggering the use of one's muscles.

Subconscious mind—works night and day, except for the deepest state of sleep (semi-superconsciousness). In the daytime it primarily works through memories and habits. At night it works primarily through dreams. In the daytime it makes records. At night it takes care of the heart, lungs, etc., like an "old janitor," and it is also the "manager-operator" of our "dream movie theater."

Superconsciousness—works in and beyond both consciousness and subconsciousness without becoming entangled in them.

Super-visions or true superconscious visions—are created by the superconscious and impregnated by Christ consciousness; they are also visions, though even more real in the sense of being solid; they may be touched, smelled, tasted, as well as seen and heard. Super-visions allow you to see and interact with saints, angels, and great spiritual masters, or true visions of the future.

Trance—an inert state on the borderland of semi-subconscious or semi-superconscious.

Visions—can be created with will and concentration and are more real, while dreams are imaginary images; visions may be had in a wakeful, open-eyed state or with closed eyes, and are created by the superconscious mind. Visions are life force projected from the brain onto the ether (somewhat like a holograph), and are not touchable.

CONCLUSION

When I awake I'll see Thy face,
When I awake I'll see Thy light.

Mother awake me from my dreams,
Mother awake me in Thy light.
Hand in hand we're dancing together,
Dancing together in Thy light.
—from the chant "When I Awake" by Swami Kriyananda

The teachings of yoga present a dynamic roadmap that clearly outlines the path from where we find ourselves at this moment to final liberation and oneness with God. Throughout this spiritual journey, most of our dreams probably are best dismissed as subconscious entertainment. Nevertheless, occasionally we may find a message in a dream which may either clarify certain signs and guideposts along our inner pathways or help us find shortcuts to speed our journey home.

Paramhansa Yogananda offers these words of advice about the Divine Dreamer (God) and this dream world in which we live: "No matter what happens, look at life with nonattachment. Consider the example of people who go to movies. The more suspenseful the plot, the more likely they are to come away saying,

'What a great movie!' If the plot was a tragedy, they may reflect, 'I am grateful. I learned so much from that story.' If the hero got caught in embarrassing situations, they may laugh appreciatively at his discomfiture. And yet, later on, when they find themselves in an embarrassing situation, are they able to laugh at the humor of it? And when tragedy strikes, are they as grateful for the lessons they learn from it? Not most of them, certainly. Their philosophy of life can be understood from the popular expression, 'Better him than me!' Be detached inwardly from whatever happens in your life. Thus, you will gradually free yourself from identification with this dream world, and become conscious of your oneness with the Dreamer."

Paramhansa Yogananda's teachings on dreams are dynamic, clear, and relevant to every aspect of daily life. Though a great yogi and mystic himself and one of the greatest yoga masters and spiritual teachers of our times, he is also careful to demystify every level of consciousness, from the lowest level of subconsciousness to the highest level of superconsciousness and cosmic consciousness. He offers effective and scientific techniques for taking charge of our consciousness, whether awake, in deep sleep, dreaming, or in the deepest meditation.

I urge you to consider studying his teachings in greater depth, for they offer shining keys to the doors to your own inner kingdom of never-ending, ever-new bliss.

My wish is that your life, including all your dreams, be filled with divine light!

In closing I hope you will enjoy this beautiful prayer-poem by Paramhansa Yogananda:

Come Into The Garden Of My Dreams

—from the *Praecepta Lessons*, Volume 1 (1934): Praeceptum #3

In the garden of my dreams grew many dream-blossoms.
The rarest flowers of my fancy all bloomed there.
Unopened buds of earthly hopes audaciously spread their petals of fulfillment,
Warmed by the light of my dreams. In the dim glow,
I spied the specters of beloved, forgotten faces, sprites of dear, dead feelings,
Long buried beneath the soil of mind, which all rose in their shining robes.
I beheld the resurrection of all experiences,
At the trumpet-call of my dream angels.

As we rest, and wake a little, to slumber again—
So from beneath the cover of fleeting dreams of birth and death,
We rise for a while and fall asleep again,
And dream another earthly dream of struggle.

On the sledge of incarnations we slide from dream to dream.
Dreaming, on a chariot of astral fire we roll from life to life.
Dreaming, we pass through dreams, failures, victories.
Dreaming, we sail over trying seas, eddies of laughter, whirlpools of
    indifference, waters of mighty events, deaths, births—dreams.

In the chamber of Thy heart I shall behold the making of the noblest dreams of life.
O Master Weaver of Dreams, teach me to make a many-hued carpet of dreams,
For all lovers of Thy pattern of dreams to walk over, as they travel to the
    Temple of Eternal Dreams.
And I will join the worshipping angels of living visions
That I may offer on Thy altar a bouquet of my newborn dreams of Thee.

ABOUT THE AUTHOR

 For over thirty-five years, Savitri Simpson has taught classes and workshops based on Paramhansa Yogananda's teachings on yoga, dreaming, the chakras, meditation, and many other related topics. She has served as a counselor, minister, and teacher at Ananda's Expanding Light Retreat Center, where she was a founder/director of the Ananda Yoga Teacher Training Program and the Ananda Meditation Teacher Training Program.

She has written several books including: *Chakras for Starters*, *The Chakras Workbook* and her two novels *Through Many Lives* and *Through the Chakras*. She has a Bachelor of Arts Degree from Baylor University. In addition to her primary devotion to yoga, meditation, and all related subjects, she is a musician, herb gardener, gourmet cook, and nature lover. She lives with her husband in a dome-home at Ananda Village near Nevada City, California.

Dear Reader,

Ananda is a worldwide work based on the same teachings expressed in this book—those of the great spiritual teacher, Paramhansa Yogananda. If you enjoyed this title, Crystal Clarity Publishers invites you to continue to deepen your spiritual life through the many avenues of Ananda Worldwide—including meditation communities, centers, and groups; online virtual community and webinars; retreat centers offering classes and teacher training in yoga and meditation; and more.

For special offers and discounts for first-time visitors to Ananda, visit:

http://www.crystalclarity.com/welcome

Feel free to contact us. We are here to serve you.

Joy to you,

Crystal Clarity Publishers

ANANDA WORLDWIDE

Ananda, a worldwide organization founded by Swami Kriyananda, offers spiritual support and resources based on the teachings of Paramhansa Yogananda. There are Ananda spiritual communities in Nevada City, Sacramento, and Palo Alto, California; Seattle, Washington; Portland and Laurelwood, Oregon; as well as a retreat center and European community in Assisi, Italy, and a community near New Delhi, India. Ananda supports more than 140 meditation groups worldwide.

For more information about Ananda's work, our communities, or meditation groups near you, please call 530.478.7560 or visit www.ananda.org.

THE EXPANDING LIGHT

The Expanding Light is the largest retreat center in the world to share exclusively the teachings of Paramhansa Yogananda. Situated in the Ananda Village community, it offers the opportunity to experience spiritual life in a contemporary ashram setting. The varied, year-round schedule of classes and programs on yoga, meditation, and spiritual practice includes Karma Yoga, Personal Retreat, Spiritual Travel, and online learning. The Ananda School of Yoga & Meditation offers certified yoga, yoga therapist, spiritual counselor, and meditation teacher trainings. Large groups are welcome.

The teaching staff are experts in Kriya Yoga meditation and all aspects of Yogananda's teachings. All staff members live at Ananda Village and bring an uplifting approach to their areas of service. The serene natural setting and delicious vegetarian meals help provide an ideal environment for a truly meaningful visit.

For more information, please call 800.346.5350
or visit www.expandinglight.org.

CRYSTAL CLARITY PUBLISHERS

Crystal Clarity Publishers offers many additional resources to assist you in your spiritual journey, including many other books (see the following pages for some of them), a wide variety of inspirational and relaxation music composed by Swami Kriyananda, and yoga and meditation videos. To request a catalog, place an order for the above products, or to find out more information, please contact us at:

Crystal Clarity Publishers / www.crystalclarity.com
14618 Tyler Foote Rd. / Nevada City, CA 95959
TOLL FREE: 800.424.1055 or 530.478.7600 / FAX: 530.478.7610
EMAIL: clarity@crystalclarity.com

For our online catalog, complete with secure ordering, please visit our website.

AUTOBIOGRAPHY OF A YOGI

Paramhansa Yogananda

Autobiography of a Yogi is one of the best-selling Eastern philosophy titles of all time, with millions of copies sold, named one of the best and most influential books of the twentieth century. This highly prized reprinting of the original 1946 edition is the only one available free from textual changes made after Yogananda's death. Yogananda was the first yoga master of India whose mission was to live and teach in the West.

In this updated edition are bonus materials, including a last chapter that Yogananda wrote in 1951, without posthumous changes. This new edition also includes the eulogy that Yogananda wrote for Gandhi, and a new foreword and afterword by Swami Kriyananda, one of Yogananda's close, direct disciples.

Also available in unabridged audiobook (MP3) format, read by Swami Kriyananda.

PARAMHANSA YOGANANDA

A Biography with Personal Reflections and Reminiscences
Swami Kriyananda

Paramhansa Yogananda's classic *Autobiography of a Yogi* is more about the saints Yogananda met than about himself—in spite of Yogananda's astonishing accomplishments.

Now, one of Yogananda's direct disciples relates the untold story of this great spiritual master and world teacher: his teenage miracles, his challenges in coming to America, his national lecture campaigns, his struggles to fulfill his world-changing mission amid incomprehension and painful betrayals, and his ultimate triumphant achievement. Kriyananda's subtle grasp of his guru's inner nature reveals Yogananda's many-sided greatness. Includes many never-before-published anecdotes.

Also available in unabridged audiobook (MP3) format, read by Swami Kriyananda.

THE NEW PATH

My Life with Paramhansa Yogananda
Swami Kriyananda

When Swami Kriyananda discovered *Autobiography of a Yogi* in 1948, he was totally new to Eastern teachings. This is a great advantage to the Western reader, since Kriyananda walks us along the yogic path as he discovers it from the moment of his initiation as a disciple of Yogananda. With winning honesty, humor, and deep insight, he shares his journey on the spiritual path through personal stories and experiences.

Through more than four hundred stories of life with Yogananda, we tune in more deeply to this great master and to the teachings he brought to the West. This book is an ideal complement to *Autobiography of a Yogi*.

The Essence of the Bhagavad Gita
Explained by Paramhansa Yogananda
As Remembered by his disciple, Swami Kriyananda

Demystifying Patanjali
The Wisdom of Paramhansa Yogananda Presented
by his direct disciple, Swami Kriyananda

The Essence of Self-Realization
The Wisdom of Paramhansa Yogananda
Recorded, Compiled, and Edited by
his disciple, Swami Kriyananda

Conversations with Yogananda
Recorded, with Reflections, by his
disciple, Swami Kriyananda

Revelations of Christ
Proclaimed by Paramhansa Yogananda
Presented by his disciple, Swami Kriyananda

Whispers from Eternity
Paramhansa Yogananda
Edited by his disciple, Swami Kriyananda

The Rubaiyat of Omar Khayyam
Paramhansa Yogananda
Edited by his disciple, Swami Kriyananda

–The Wisdom of Yogananda series–
How To Be Happy All the Time
Karma and Reincarnation
Spiritual Relationships
How To Be a Success
How To Have Courage, Calmness, and Confidence
How To Achieve Glowing Health and Vitality

Meditation for Starters with CD
Swami Kriyananda

Intuition for Starters
Swami Kriyananda

Chakras for Starters
Savitri Simpson

Vegetarian Cooking for Starters
Diksha McCord

The Art and Science of Raja Yoga
Swami Kriyananda

Awaken to Superconsciousness
Swami Kriyananda

Living Wisely, Living Well
Swami Kriyananda

The Bhagavad Gita
According to Paramhansa Yogananda
Edited by his disciple, Swami Kriyananda

How to Meditate
Jyotish Novak

Self-Expansion Through Marriage
Swami Kriyananda

The Time Tunnel
Swami Kriyananda

The Yugas
Joseph Selbie & David Steinmetz

God Is for Everyone
Inspired by Paramhansa Yogananda
As taught to and understood by his
disciple, Swami Kriyananda

Religion in the New Age
Swami Kriyananda

The Art of Supportive Leadership
J. Donald Walters (Swami Kriyananda)

Money Magnetism
J. Donald Walters (Swami Kriyananda)

Two Souls: Four Lives
Catherine Kairavi

In Divine Friendship
Swami Kriyananda

30-Day Essentials for Marriage
Jyotish Novak

30-Day Essentials for Career
Jyotish Novak

Education for Life
J. Donald Walters (Swami Kriyananda)

The Peace Treaty
J. Donald Walters (Swami Kriyananda)

Pilgrimage to Guadalupe
Swami Kriyananda

Love Perfected, Life Divine
Swami Kriyananda